D1712515

This Book Belongs To:

_____

EMAIL: _____

PHONE #: _____

WEBSITE: _____

SOCIAL MEDIA: _____

INDEX

Page #	First & last name	Email address

INDEX

Page #	First & last name	Email address

INDEX

Page #	First & last name	Email address

INDEX

Page #	First & last name	Email address

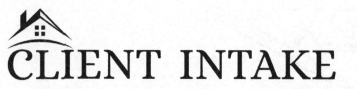

CLIENT INTAKE

Date: _____

Time frame for selling/buying/renting?
_____

☐ **Buyer**   ☐ **Seller**   ☐ **Renter**   (1)

First & last name: _____

Contact number: _____ Home/other: _____

Mailing address: _____

Email address: _____

Property of interest: _____ (MLS#   )

If buying, are you pre-approved? _____ If, yes, with whom? _____

Lead source: ☐ Social media   ☐ Craigslist

☐ Website   ☐ Billboard sign

☐ Newspaper/magazine AD   ☐ Real estate review book

☐ Referref by client | past client | family | friend: _____

What type of property are interested in?

☐ LAND/LOTS/ACERAGE   ☐ RESIDENTIAL   ☐ COMMERCIAL   ☐ INVESTMENT

type of land? acres? aprovements? water? sewer? electric? | *sq ft # of beds/ baths acres?* | *type of building? sq ft? how many rooms? improvements?* | *type of property? single or multi family home? duplex? 4-plex?*

_____

_____

_____

_____

ANY ADDITIONAL INFO:

_____

_____

_____

_____

CLIENT INTAKE

Date: _____

Time frame for selling/buying/renting?

_____

☐ **Buyer**　　　☐ **Seller**　　　☐ **Renter**　　　(2)

First & last name: _____

Contact number: _____ Home/other: _____

Mailing address: _____

Email address: _____

Property of interest: _____ (MLS# _____)

If buying, are you pre-approved? _____ If, yes, with whom? _____

Lead source:　☐ Social media　　　　☐ Craigslist

☐ Website　　　　☐ Billboard sign

☐ Newspaper/magazine AD　　☐ Real estate review book

☐ Referref by client | past client | family | friend: _____

What type of property are interested in?

☐ LAND/LOTS/ACERAGE　　☐ RESIDENTIAL　　☐ COMMERCIAL　　☐ INVESTMENT

type of land? acres? aprovements? water? sewer? electric?　　*sq ft # of beds/ baths acres?*　　*type of building? sq ft? how many rooms? improvements?*　　*type of property? single or multi family home? duplex? 4-plex?*

_____

_____

_____

_____

ANY ADDITIONAL INFO:

_____

_____

_____

_____

CLIENT INTAKE

Date: _____

Time frame for selling/buying/renting?

_____

☐ **Buyer**　　　☐ **Seller**　　　☐ **Renter**　　3

First & last name: _____

Contact number: _____ Home/other: _____

Mailing address: _____

Email address: _____

Property of interest: _____ (MLS#　　　　)

If buying, are you pre-approved? _____ If, yes, with whom? _____

Lead source:　　☐ Social media　　　　　☐ Craigslist

　　　　　　　　　☐ Website　　　　　　　☐ Billboard sign

　　　　　　　　　☐ Newspaper/magazine AD　☐ Real estate review book

　　　　　　　　　☐ Referref by client | past client | family | friend: _____

What type of property are interested in?

☐ LAND/LOTS/ACERAGE　　☐ RESIDENTIAL　　☐ COMMERCIAL　　☐ INVESTMENT

type of land? acres? aprovements? water? sewer? electric?　　sq ft # of beds/ baths acres?　　type of building? sq ft? how many rooms? improvements?　　type of property? single or multi family home? duplex? 4-plex?

_____

_____

_____

_____

ANY ADDITIONAL INFO:

_____

_____

_____

_____

CLIENT INTAKE

Date: _____

Time frame for selling/buying/renting?
_____

☐ **Buyer**   ☐ **Seller**   ☐ **Renter**   (4)

First & last name: _____

Contact number: _____ Home/other: _____

Mailing address: _____

Email address: _____

Property of interest: _____ (MLS# _____)

If buying, are you pre-approved? _____ If, yes, with whom? _____

Lead source: ☐ Social media   ☐ Craigslist

☐ Website   ☐ Billboard sign

☐ Newspaper/magazine AD   ☐ Real estate review book

☐ Referref by client | past client | family | friend: _____

What type of property are interested in?

☐ LAND/LOTS/ACERAGE   ☐ RESIDENTIAL   ☐ COMMERCIAL   ☐ INVESTMENT

type of land? acres? aprovements?   *sq ft # of beds/ baths acres?*   *type of building? sq ft?*   *type of property? single or multi*
water? sewer? electric?   *how many rooms? improvements?*   *family home? duplex? 4-plex?*

_____

_____

_____

_____

ANY ADDITIONAL INFO:

_____

_____

_____

_____

CLIENT INTAKE

Date: _____

Time frame for selling/buying/renting?

_____

☐ **Buyer**   ☐ **Seller**   ☐ **Renter**   5

First & last name: _____

Contact number: _____ Home/other: _____

Mailing address: _____

Email address: _____

Property of interest: _____ (MLS#   )

If buying, are you pre-approved? _____ If, yes, with whom? _____

Lead source: ☐ Social media   ☐ Craigslist

☐ Website   ☐ Billboard sign

☐ Newspaper/magazine AD   ☐ Real estate review book

☐ Referref by client | past client | family | friend: _____

What type of property are interested in?

☐ LAND/LOTS/ACERAGE   ☐ RESIDENTIAL   ☐ COMMERCIAL   ☐ INVESTMENT

type of land? acres? aprovements? water? sewer? electric?

sq ft # of beds/ baths acres?

type of building? sq ft? how many rooms? improvements?

type of property? single or multi family home? duplex? 4-plex?

_____

_____

_____

_____

ANY ADDITIONAL INFO:

_____

_____

_____

_____

CLIENT INTAKE

Date: _____

Time frame for selling/buying/renting?
_____

☐ **Buyer**   ☐ **Seller**   ☐ **Renter**   ⬤ 6

First & last name: _____

Contact number: _____ Home/other: _____

Mailing address: _____

Email address: _____

Property of interest: _____ (MLS# _____)

If buying, are you pre-approved? _____ If, yes, with whom? _____

Lead source:
☐ Social media   ☐ Craigslist

☐ Website   ☐ Billboard sign

☐ Newspaper/magazine AD ☐ Real estate review book

☐ Referref by client | past client | family | friend: _____

What type of property are interested in?

☐ LAND/LOTS/ACERAGE   ☐ RESIDENTIAL   ☐ COMMERCIAL   ☐ INVESTMENT

type of land? acres? aprovements? water? sewer? electric? *sq ft # of beds/ baths acres?* *type of building? sq ft? how many rooms? improvements?* *type of property? single or multi family home? duplex? 4-plex?*

_____

_____

_____

_____

ANY ADDITIONAL INFO:

_____

_____

_____

_____

CLIENT INTAKE

Date: _____

Time frame for selling/buying/renting?
_____

☐ **Buyer**   ☐ **Seller**   ☐ **Renter**   7

First & last name: _____

Contact number: _____ Home/other: _____

Mailing address: _____

Email address: _____

Property of interest: _____ (MLS# ____)

If buying, are you pre-approved? _____ If, yes, with whom? _____

Lead source:

☐ Social media   ☐ Craigslist

☐ Website   ☐ Billboard sign

☐ Newspaper/magazine AD   ☐ Real estate review book

☐ Referref by client | past client | family | friend: _____

What type of property are interested in?

☐ LAND/LOTS/ACERAGE   ☐ RESIDENTIAL   ☐ COMMERCIAL   ☐ INVESTMENT

type of land? acres? aprovements? water? sewer? electric?   *sq ft # of beds/ baths acres?*   *type of building? sq ft? how many rooms? improvements?*   *type of property? single or multi family home? duplex? 4-plex?*

_____

_____

_____

_____

ANY ADDITIONAL INFO:

_____

_____

_____

_____

CLIENT INTAKE

Date: _____

Time frame for selling/buying/renting?
_____

☐ **Buyer**   ☐ **Seller**   ☐ **Renter**   8

First & last name: _____

Contact number: _____ Home/other: _____

Mailing address: _____

Email address: _____

Property of interest: _____ (MLS#   )

If buying, are you pre-approved? _____ If, yes, with whom? _____

Lead source: ☐ Social media   ☐ Craigslist

☐ Website   ☐ Billboard sign

☐ Newspaper/magazine AD   ☐ Real estate review book

☐ Referref by client | past client | family | friend: _____

What type of property are interested in?

☐ LAND/LOTS/ACERAGE   ☐ RESIDENTIAL   ☐ COMMERCIAL   ☐ INVESTMENT

type of land? acres? aprovements?
water? sewer? electric?

sq ft # of beds/ baths acres?

type of building? sq ft?
how many rooms? improvements?

type of property? single or multi
family home? duplex? 4-plex?

_____

_____

_____

_____

ANY ADDITIONAL INFO:

_____

_____

_____

_____

CLIENT INTAKE

Date: _____

Time frame for selling/buying/renting?
_____

☐ **Buyer**　　☐ **Seller**　　☐ **Renter**　　9

First & last name: _____

Contact number: _____ Home/other: _____

Mailing address: _____

Email address: _____

Property of interest: _____ (MLS# _____)

If buying, are you pre-approved? _____ If, yes, with whom? _____

Lead source:　☐ Social media　　　☐ Craigslist

　　　　　　　☐ Website　　　　　☐ Billboard sign

　　　　　　　☐ Newspaper/magazine AD　☐ Real estate review book

　　　　　　　☐ Referref by client | past client | family | friend: _____

What type of property are interested in?

☐ LAND/LOTS/ACERAGE　☐ RESIDENTIAL　☐ COMMERCIAL　☐ INVESTMENT

type of land? acres? aprovements? water? sewer? electric?　sq ft # of beds/ baths acres?　type of building? sq ft? how many rooms? improvements?　type of property? single or multi family home? duplex? 4-plex?

_____

_____

_____

_____

ANY ADDITIONAL INFO:

_____

_____

_____

CLIENT INTAKE

Date: _____

Time frame for selling/buying/renting?
_____

☐ **Buyer**   ☐ **Seller**   ☐ **Renter**   10

First & last name: _____

Contact number: _____ Home/other: _____

Mailing address: _____

Email address: _____

Property of interest: _____ (MLS# _____)

If buying, are you pre-approved? _____ If, yes, with whom? _____

Lead source: ☐ Social media   ☐ Craigslist

☐ Website   ☐ Billboard sign

☐ Newspaper/magazine AD   ☐ Real estate review book

☐ Referref by client | past client | family | friend: _____

What type of property are interested in?

☐ LAND/LOTS/ACERAGE   ☐ RESIDENTIAL   ☐ COMMERCIAL   ☐ INVESTMENT

type of land? acres? aprovements? water? sewer? electric?   *sq ft # of beds/ baths acres?*   *type of building? sq ft? how many rooms? improvements?*   *type of property? single or multi family home? duplex? 4-plex?*

_____

_____

_____

_____

ANY ADDITIONAL INFO:

_____

_____

_____

_____

CLIENT INTAKE

Date: _____

Time frame for selling/buying/renting?

_____

☐ **Buyer**   ☐ **Seller**   ☐ **Renter**   11

First & last name: _____

Contact number: _____ Home/other: _____

Mailing address: _____

Email address: _____

Property of interest: _____ (MLS#   )

If buying, are you pre-approved? _____ If, yes, with whom? _____

Lead source: ☐ Social media   ☐ Craigslist

☐ Website   ☐ Billboard sign

☐ Newspaper/magazine AD   ☐ Real estate review book

☐ Referref by client | past client | family | friend: _____

What type of property are interested in?

☐ LAND/LOTS/ACERAGE   ☐ RESIDENTIAL   ☐ COMMERCIAL   ☐ INVESTMENT

type of land? acres? aprovements? water? sewer? electric?   *sq ft # of beds/ baths acres?*   *type of building? sq ft? how many rooms? improvements?*   *type of property? single or multi family home? duplex? 4-plex?*

_____

_____

_____

_____

ANY ADDITIONAL INFO:

_____

_____

_____

_____

CLIENT INTAKE

Date: _____

Time frame for selling/buying/renting?
_____

☐ **Buyer** ☐ **Seller** ☐ **Renter** ⬭ 12

First & last name: _____

Contact number: _____ Home/other: _____

Mailing address: _____

Email address: _____

Property of interest: _____ (MLS#_____)

If buying, are you pre-approved? _____ If, yes, with whom? _____

Lead source: ☐ Social media   ☐ Craigslist

☐ Website   ☐ Billboard sign

☐ Newspaper/magazine AD   ☐ Real estate review book

☐ Referref by client | past client | family | friend: _____

What type of property are interested in?

☐ LAND/LOTS/ACERAGE   ☐ RESIDENTIAL   ☐ COMMERCIAL   ☐ INVESTMENT

type of land? acres? aprovements? water? sewer? electric?   *sq ft # of beds/ baths acres?*   *type of building? sq ft? how many rooms? improvements?*   *type of property? single or multi family home? duplex? 4-plex?*

_____

_____

_____

_____

ANY ADDITIONAL INFO:

_____

_____

_____

_____

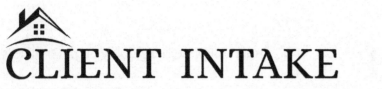

CLIENT INTAKE

Date: _____

Time frame for selling/buying/renting?

_____

☐ **Buyer**   ☐ **Seller**   ☐ **Renter**   13

First & last name: _____

Contact number: _____ Home/other: _____

Mailing address: _____

Email address: _____

Property of interest: _____ (MLS#_____)

If buying, are you pre-approved? _____ If, yes, with whom? _____

Lead source:
☐ Social media   ☐ Craigslist

☐ Website   ☐ Billboard sign

☐ Newspaper/magazine AD ☐ Real estate review book

☐ Referref by client | past client | family | friend: _____

What type of property are interested in?

☐ LAND/LOTS/ACERAGE	☐ RESIDENTIAL	☐ COMMERCIAL	☐ INVESTMENT
type of land? acres? aprovements? water? sewer? electric?	sq ft # of beds/ baths acres?	type of building? sq ft? how many rooms? improvements?	type of property? single or multi family home? duplex? 4-plex?

_____

_____

_____

_____

ANY ADDITIONAL INFO:

_____

_____

_____

_____

CLIENT INTAKE

Date: _____

Time frame for selling/buying/renting?
_____

☐ **Buyer**   ☐ **Seller**   ☐ **Renter**   14

First & last name: _____

Contact number: _____ Home/other: _____

Mailing address: _____

Email address: _____

Property of interest: _____ (MLS#   )

If buying, are you pre-approved? _____ If, yes, with whom? _____

Lead source:

☐ Social media   ☐ Craigslist

☐ Website   ☐ Billboard sign

☐ Newspaper/magazine AD ☐ Real estate review book

☐ Referref by client | past client | family | friend: _____

What type of property are interested in?

☐ LAND/LOTS/ACERAGE   ☐ RESIDENTIAL   ☐ COMMERCIAL   ☐ INVESTMENT

type of land? acres? aprovements? water? sewer? electric? | *sq ft # of beds/ baths acres?* | *type of building? sq ft? how many rooms? improvements?* | *type of property? single or multi family home? duplex? 4-plex?*

_____

_____

_____

_____

ANY ADDITIONAL INFO:

_____

_____

_____

_____

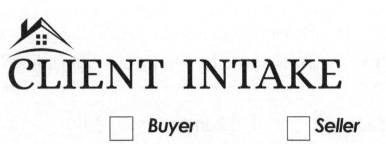

CLIENT INTAKE

Date: _____

Time frame for selling/buying/renting?
_____

☐ **Buyer**　　　☐ **Seller**　　　☐ **Renter**　　　15

First & last name: _____

Contact number: _____ Home/other: _____

Mailing address: _____

Email address: _____

Property of interest: _____ (MLS# _____)

If buying, are you pre-approved? _____ If, yes, with whom? _____

Lead source:　☐ Social media　　　　　　☐ Craigslist

☐ Website　　　　　　☐ Billboard sign

☐ Newspaper/magazine AD　　☐ Real estate review book

☐ Referref by client | past client | family | friend: _____

What type of property are interested in?

☐ LAND/LOTS/ACERAGE　　☐ RESIDENTIAL　　☐ COMMERCIAL　　☐ INVESTMENT

type of land? acres? aprovements? water? sewer? electric?　　sq ft # of beds/ baths acres?　　type of building? sq ft? how many rooms? improvements?　　type of property? single or multi family home? duplex? 4-plex?

_____

_____

_____

_____

ANY ADDITIONAL INFO:

_____

_____

_____

_____

CLIENT INTAKE

Date: _____

Time frame for selling/buying/renting?
_____

☐ **Buyer**　　　☐ **Seller**　　　☐ **Renter**　　　16

First & last name: _____

Contact number: _____ Home/other: _____

Mailing address: _____

Email address: _____

Property of interest: _____ (MLS#　　　)

If buying, are you pre-approved? _____ If, yes, with whom? _____

Lead source:
☐ Social media　　　　　　　☐ Craigslist

☐ Website　　　　　　　　　☐ Billboard sign

☐ Newspaper/magazine AD　　☐ Real estate review book

☐ Referref by client | past client | family | friend: _____

What type of property are interested in?

☐ LAND/LOTS/ACERAGE　　☐ RESIDENTIAL　　☐ COMMERCIAL　　☐ INVESTMENT

type of land? acres? aprovements?　sq ft # of beds/ baths acres?　type of building? sq ft?　type of property? single or multi
water? sewer? electric?　　　　　　　　　　　　　　　how many rooms? improvements?　family home? duplex? 4-plex?

_____

_____

_____

_____

ANY ADDITIONAL INFO:

_____

_____

_____

_____

CLIENT INTAKE

Date: _____

Time frame for selling/buying/renting?

_____

☐ **Buyer**   ☐ **Seller**   ☐ **Renter**   17

First & last name: _____

Contact number: _____ Home/other: _____

Mailing address: _____

Email address: _____

Property of interest: _____ (MLS#   )

If buying, are you pre-approved? _____ If, yes, with whom? _____

Lead source: ☐ Social media   ☐ Craigslist

☐ Website   ☐ Billboard sign

☐ Newspaper/magazine AD   ☐ Real estate review book

☐ Referref by client | past client | family | friend: _____

What type of property are interested in?

☐ *LAND/LOTS/ACERAGE*   ☐ *RESIDENTIAL*   ☐ *COMMERCIAL*   ☐ *INVESTMENT*

type of land? acres? aprovements?   *sq ft # of beds/ baths acres?*   *type of building? sq ft?*   *type of property? single or multi*
water? sewer? electric?   *how many rooms? improvements?*   *family home? duplex? 4-plex?*

_____

_____

_____

_____

ANY ADDITIONAL INFO:

_____

_____

_____

_____

CLIENT INTAKE

Date: _____

Time frame for selling/buying/renting?

_____

☐ **Buyer**　　☐ **Seller**　　☐ **Renter**　　(18)

First & last name: _____

Contact number: _____ Home/other: _____

Mailing address: _____

Email address: _____

Property of interest: _____ (MLS# ___)

If buying, are you pre-approved? _____ If, yes, with whom? _____

Lead source:
☐ Social media　　　　　☐ Craigslist

☐ Website　　　　　　　☐ Billboard sign

☐ Newspaper/magazine AD　☐ Real estate review book

☐ Referref by client | past client | family | friend: _____

What type of property are interested in?

☐ LAND/LOTS/ACERAGE

type of land? acres? aprovements? water? sewer? electric?

☐ RESIDENTIAL

sq ft # of beds/ baths acres?

☐ COMMERCIAL

type of building? sq ft? how many rooms? improvements?

☐ INVESTMENT

type of property? single or multi family home? duplex? 4-plex?

_____

_____

_____

_____

ANY ADDITIONAL INFO:

_____

_____

_____

_____

CLIENT INTAKE

Date: _____

Time frame for selling/buying/renting?
_____

☐ **Buyer**　　☐ **Seller**　　☐ **Renter**　　19

First & last name: _____

Contact number: _____ Home/other: _____

Mailing address: _____

Email address: _____

Property of interest: _____ (MLS# _____)

If buying, are you pre-approved? _____ If, yes, with whom? _____

Lead source:
☐ Social media　　　　　　☐ Craigslist

☐ Website　　　　　　　　☐ Billboard sign

☐ Newspaper/magazine AD　☐ Real estate review book

☐ Referref by client | past client | family | friend: _____

What type of property are interested in?

☐ LAND/LOTS/ACERAGE　☐ RESIDENTIAL　☐ COMMERCIAL　☐ INVESTMENT

type of land? acres? aprovements? water? sewer? electric?　*sq ft # of beds/ baths acres?*　*type of building? sq ft? how many rooms? improvements?*　*type of property? single or multi family home? duplex? 4-plex?*

_____

_____

_____

_____

ANY ADDITIONAL INFO:

_____

_____

_____

_____

CLIENT INTAKE

Date: _____

Time frame for selling/buying/renting?

_____

☐ **Buyer**   ☐ **Seller**   ☐ **Renter**   20

First & last name: _____

Contact number: _____ Home/other: _____

Mailing address: _____

Email address: _____

Property of interest: _____ (MLS#   )

If buying, are you pre-approved? _____ If, yes, with whom? _____

Lead source: ☐ Social media   ☐ Craigslist

☐ Website   ☐ Billboard sign

☐ Newspaper/magazine AD   ☐ Real estate review book

☐ Referref by client | past client | family | friend: _____

What type of property are interested in?

☐ LAND/LOTS/ACERAGE   ☐ RESIDENTIAL   ☐ COMMERCIAL   ☐ INVESTMENT

type of land? acres? aprovements? water? sewer? electric?   *sq ft # of beds/ baths acres?*   *type of building? sq ft? how many rooms? improvements?*   *type of property? single or multi family home? duplex? 4-plex?*

_____

_____

_____

_____

ANY ADDITIONAL INFO:

_____

_____

_____

_____

CLIENT INTAKE

Date: _____

Time frame for selling/buying/renting?

_____

☐ **Buyer**　　　☐ **Seller**　　　☐ **Renter**　　　21

First & last name: _____

Contact number: _____ Home/other: _____

Mailing address: _____

Email address: _____

Property of interest: _____ (MLS# _____)

If buying, are you pre-approved? _____ If, yes, with whom? _____

Lead source:
☐ Social media ☐ Craigslist

☐ Website ☐ Billboard sign

☐ Newspaper/magazine AD ☐ Real estate review book

☐ Referref by client | past client | family | friend: _____

What type of property are interested in?

☐ LAND/LOTS/ACERAGE ☐ RESIDENTIAL ☐ COMMERCIAL ☐ INVESTMENT

type of land? acres? aprovements? water? sewer? electric?　　sq ft # of beds/ baths acres?　　type of building? sq ft? how many rooms? improvements?　　type of property? single or multi family home? duplex? 4-plex?

_____

_____

_____

_____

ANY ADDITIONAL INFO:

_____

_____

_____

_____

CLIENT INTAKE

Date: _____

Time frame for selling/buying/renting?

_____

☐ **Buyer**　　　☐ **Seller**　　　☐ **Renter**　　　22

First & last name: _____

Contact number: _____ Home/other: _____

Mailing address: _____

Email address: _____

Property of interest: _____ (MLS# _____)

If buying, are you pre-approved? _____ If, yes, with whom? _____

Lead source:
☐ Social media　　　　　☐ Craigslist

☐ Website　　　　　　　☐ Billboard sign

☐ Newspaper/magazine AD　☐ Real estate review book

☐ Referref by client | past client | family | friend: _____

What type of property are interested in?

☐ LAND/LOTS/ACERAGE　　☐ RESIDENTIAL　　☐ COMMERCIAL　　☐ INVESTMENT

type of land? acres? aprovements? water? sewer? electric?　　*sq ft # of beds/ baths acres?*　　*type of building? sq ft? how many rooms? improvements?*　　*type of property? single or multi family home? duplex? 4-plex?*

_____

_____

_____

_____

ANY ADDITIONAL INFO:

_____

_____

_____

_____

CLIENT INTAKE

Date: _____

Time frame for selling/buying/renting?

_____

☐ **Buyer**　　　☐ **Seller**　　　☐ **Renter**　　　23

First & last name: _____

Contact number: _____ Home/other: _____

Mailing address: _____

Email address: _____

Property of interest: _____ (MLS# _____)

If buying, are you pre-approved? _____ If, yes, with whom? _____

Lead source:　
☐ Social media　　　　　　☐ Craigslist

☐ Website　　　　　　　　☐ Billboard sign

☐ Newspaper/magazine AD　☐ Real estate review book

☐ Referref by client | past client | family | friend: _____

What type of property are interested in?

☐ LAND/LOTS/ACERAGE　☐ RESIDENTIAL　☐ COMMERCIAL　☐ INVESTMENT

type of land? acres? aprovements? water? sewer? electric?　　sq ft # of beds/ baths acres?　　type of building? sq ft? how many rooms? improvements?　　type of property? single or multi family home? duplex? 4-plex?

_____

_____

_____

_____

ANY ADDITIONAL INFO:

_____

_____

_____

_____

CLIENT INTAKE

Date: _____

Time frame for selling/buying/renting?

_____

☐ **Buyer**　　　☐ **Seller**　　　☐ **Renter**　　　24

First & last name: _____

Contact number: _____ Home/other: _____

Mailing address: _____

Email address: _____

Property of interest: _____ (MLS#_____)

If buying, are you pre-approved? _____ If, yes, with whom? _____

Lead source:

☐ Social media　　　　　　☐ Craigslist

☐ Website　　　　　　　　☐ Billboard sign

☐ Newspaper/magazine AD　☐ Real estate review book

☐ Referref by client | past client | family | friend: _____

What type of property are interested in?

☐ LAND/LOTS/ACERAGE　☐ RESIDENTIAL　☐ COMMERCIAL　☐ INVESTMENT

type of land? acres? aprovements? water? sewer? electric?　　*sq ft # of beds/ baths acres?*　　*type of building? sq ft? how many rooms? improvements?*　　*type of property? single or multi family home? duplex? 4-plex?*

_____

_____

_____

_____

ANY ADDITIONAL INFO:

_____

_____

_____

_____

CLIENT INTAKE

Date: _____

Time frame for selling/buying/renting?
_____

☐ **Buyer**　　　☐ **Seller**　　　☐ **Renter**　　25

First & last name: _____

Contact number: _____ Home/other: _____

Mailing address: _____

Email address: _____

Property of interest: _____ (MLS# _____)

If buying, are you pre-approved? _____ If, yes, with whom? _____

Lead source:　　☐ Social media　　　　　☐ Craigslist

　　　　　　　　☐ Website　　　　　　　☐ Billboard sign

　　　　　　　　☐ Newspaper/magazine AD　　☐ Real estate review book

　　　　　　　　☐ Referref by client | past client | family | friend: _____

What type of property are interested in?

☐ LAND/LOTS/ACERAGE　　☐ RESIDENTIAL　　☐ COMMERCIAL　　☐ INVESTMENT

type of land? acres? aprovements? water? sewer? electric?　　sq ft # of beds/ baths acres?　　type of building? sq ft? how many rooms? improvements?　　type of property? single or multi family home? duplex? 4-plex?

_____

_____

_____

_____

ANY ADDITIONAL INFO:

_____

_____

_____

_____

CLIENT INTAKE

Date: _____

Time frame for selling/buying/renting?
_____

☐ **Buyer**   ☐ **Seller**   ☐ **Renter**   26

First & last name: _____

Contact number: _____ Home/other: _____

Mailing address: _____

Email address: _____

Property of interest: _____ (MLS# _____)

If buying, are you pre-approved? _____ If, yes, with whom? _____

Lead source:
☐ Social media   ☐ Craigslist

☐ Website   ☐ Billboard sign

☐ Newspaper/magazine AD   ☐ Real estate review book

☐ Referref by client | past client | family | friend: _____

What type of property are interested in?

☐ LAND/LOTS/ACERAGE
type of land? acres? aprovements? water? sewer? electric?

☐ RESIDENTIAL
sq ft # of beds/ baths acres?

☐ COMMERCIAL
type of building? sq ft? how many rooms? improvements?

☐ INVESTMENT
type of property? single or multi family home? duplex? 4-plex?

_____
_____
_____
_____

ANY ADDITIONAL INFO:

_____
_____
_____
_____

CLIENT INTAKE

Date: _____

Time frame for selling/buying/renting?
_____

☐ **Buyer**   ☐ **Seller**   ☐ **Renter**   27

First & last name: _____

Contact number: _____ Home/other: _____

Mailing address: _____

Email address: _____

Property of interest: _____ (MLS# _____)

If buying, are you pre-approved? _____ If, yes, with whom? _____

Lead source:
☐ Social media   ☐ Craigslist

☐ Website   ☐ Billboard sign

☐ Newspaper/magazine AD ☐ Real estate review book

☐ Referref by client | past client | family | friend: _____

What type of property are interested in?

☐ LAND/LOTS/ACERAGE   ☐ RESIDENTIAL   ☐ COMMERCIAL   ☐ INVESTMENT

type of land? acres? aprovements? water? sewer? electric?   *sq ft # of beds/ baths acres?*   *type of building? sq ft? how many rooms? improvements?*   *type of property? single or multi family home? duplex? 4-plex?*

_____

_____

_____

_____

ANY ADDITIONAL INFO:

_____

_____

_____

_____

CLIENT INTAKE

Date: _____

Time frame for selling/buying/renting?

_____

☐ **Buyer**　　　☐ **Seller**　　　☐ **Renter**　　　28

First & last name: _____

Contact number: _____ Home/other: _____

Mailing address: _____

Email address: _____

Property of interest: _____ (MLS# _____)

If buying, are you pre-approved? _____ If, yes, with whom? _____

Lead source:　☐ Social media　　　　　☐ Craigslist

　　　　　　　☐ Website　　　　　　　☐ Billboard sign

　　　　　　　☐ Newspaper/magazine AD　☐ Real estate review book

　　　　　　　☐ Referref by client | past client | family | friend: _____

What type of property are interested in?

☐ LAND/LOTS/ACERAGE　☐ RESIDENTIAL　☐ COMMERCIAL　☐ INVESTMENT

type of land? acres? aprovements? water? sewer? electric?　　*sq ft # of beds/ baths acres?*　　*type of building? sq ft? how many rooms? improvements?*　　*type of property? single or multi family home? duplex? 4-plex?*

_____

_____

_____

_____

ANY ADDITIONAL INFO:

_____

_____

_____

_____

CLIENT INTAKE

Date: _____

Time frame for selling/buying/renting?

_____

☐ **Buyer**   ☐ **Seller**   ☐ **Renter**   29

First & last name: _____

Contact number: _____ Home/other: _____

Mailing address: _____

Email address: _____

Property of interest: _____ (MLS#_____)

If buying, are you pre-approved? _____ If, yes, with whom? _____

Lead source: ☐ Social media   ☐ Craigslist

☐ Website   ☐ Billboard sign

☐ Newspaper/magazine AD   ☐ Real estate review book

☐ Referref by client | past client | family | friend: _____

What type of property are interested in?

☐ LAND/LOTS/ACERAGE   ☐ RESIDENTIAL   ☐ COMMERCIAL   ☐ INVESTMENT

type of land? acres? aprovements? water? sewer? electric?   sq ft # of beds/ baths acres?   type of building? sq ft? how many rooms? improvements?   type of property? single or multi family home? duplex? 4-plex?

_____

_____

_____

_____

ANY ADDITIONAL INFO:

_____

_____

_____

CLIENT INTAKE

Date: _____

Time frame for selling/buying/renting?

_____

☐ **Buyer**   ☐ **Seller**   ☐ **Renter**   30

First & last name: _____

Contact number: _____ Home/other: _____

Mailing address: _____

Email address: _____

Property of interest: _____ (MLS# _____)

If buying, are you pre-approved? _____ If, yes, with whom? _____

Lead source: ☐ Social media   ☐ Craigslist

                   ☐ Website   ☐ Billboard sign

                   ☐ Newspaper/magazine AD ☐ Real estate review book

                   ☐ Referref by client | past client | family | friend: _____

What type of property are interested in?

☐ LAND/LOTS/ACERAGE   ☐ RESIDENTIAL   ☐ COMMERCIAL   ☐ INVESTMENT

type of land? acres? aprovements?   *sq ft # of beds/ baths acres?*   *type of building? sq ft?*   *type of property? single or multi*
water? sewer? electric?   *how many rooms? improvements?*   *family home? duplex? 4-plex?*

_____

_____

_____

_____

ANY ADDITIONAL INFO:

_____

_____

_____

_____

CLIENT INTAKE

Date: _____

Time frame for selling/buying/renting?
_____

☐ **Buyer**　　　☐ **Seller**　　　☐ **Renter**　　　31

First & last name: _____

Contact number: _____ Home/other: _____

Mailing address: _____

Email address: _____

Property of interest: _____ (MLS# ____)

If buying, are you pre-approved? _____ If, yes, with whom? _____

Lead source:　☐ Social media　　　　　☐ Craigslist

　　　　　　　　☐ Website　　　　　　　☐ Billboard sign

　　　　　　　　☐ Newspaper/magazine AD　☐ Real estate review book

　　　　　　　　☐ Referref by client | past client | family | friend: _____

What type of property are interested in?

☐ LAND/LOTS/ACERAGE　　☐ RESIDENTIAL　　☐ COMMERCIAL　　☐ INVESTMENT

type of land? acres? aprovements?　sq ft # of beds/ baths acres?　type of building? sq ft?　type of property? single or multi
water? sewer? electric?　　　　　　　　　　　　　　how many rooms? improvements?　family home? duplex? 4-plex?

_____

_____

_____

_____

ANY ADDITIONAL INFO:

_____

_____

_____

CLIENT INTAKE

Date: _____

Time frame for selling/buying/renting?
_____

☐ **Buyer**　　　☐ **Seller**　　　☐ **Renter**　　　32

First & last name: _____

Contact number: _____ Home/other: _____

Mailing address: _____

Email address: _____

Property of interest: _____ (MLS#　　　　)

If buying, are you pre-approved? _____ If, yes, with whom? _____

Lead source:　　☐ Social media　　　　　☐ Craigslist

☐ Website　　　　　　　　　　　☐ Billboard sign

☐ Newspaper/magazine AD　　　☐ Real estate review book

☐ Referref by client | past client | family | friend: _____

What type of property are interested in?

☐ LAND/LOTS/ACERAGE　　☐ RESIDENTIAL　　☐ COMMERCIAL　　☐ INVESTMENT

type of land? acres? aprovements? water? sewer? electric?　　sq ft # of beds/ baths acres?　　type of building? sq ft? how many rooms? improvements?　　type of property? single or multi family home? duplex? 4-plex?

_____

_____

_____

_____

ANY ADDITIONAL INFO:

_____

_____

_____

_____

CLIENT INTAKE

Date: _____

Time frame for selling/buying/renting?

_____

☐ **Buyer**   ☐ **Seller**   ☐ **Renter**   33

First & last name: _____

Contact number: _____ Home/other: _____

Mailing address: _____

Email address: _____

Property of interest: _____ (MLS#   )

If buying, are you pre-approved? _____ If, yes, with whom? _____

Lead source:

☐ Social media   ☐ Craigslist

☐ Website   ☐ Billboard sign

☐ Newspaper/magazine AD   ☐ Real estate review book

☐ Referref by client | past client | family | friend: _____

What type of property are interested in?

☐ LAND/LOTS/ACERAGE

type of land? acres? aprovements? water? sewer? electric?

☐ RESIDENTIAL

sq ft # of beds/ baths acres?

☐ COMMERCIAL

type of building? sq ft? how many rooms? improvements?

☐ INVESTMENT

type of property? single or multi family home? duplex? 4-plex?

_____

_____

_____

_____

ANY ADDITIONAL INFO:

_____

_____

_____

_____

CLIENT INTAKE

Date: _____

Time frame for selling/buying/renting?
_____

☐ **Buyer** ☐ **Seller** ☐ **Renter** 34

First & last name: _____

Contact number: _____ Home/other: _____

Mailing address: _____

Email address: _____

Property of interest: _____ (MLS# _____)

If buying, are you pre-approved? _____ If, yes, with whom? _____

Lead source: ☐ Social media   ☐ Craigslist

☐ Website   ☐ Billboard sign

☐ Newspaper/magazine AD   ☐ Real estate review book

☐ Referref by client | past client | family | friend: _____

What type of property are interested in?

☐ LAND/LOTS/ACERAGE ☐ RESIDENTIAL ☐ COMMERCIAL ☐ INVESTMENT

type of land? acres? aprovements? water? sewer? electric? | *sq ft # of beds/ baths acres?* | *type of building? sq ft? how many rooms? improvements?* | *type of property? single or multi family home? duplex? 4-plex?*

_____
_____
_____
_____

ANY ADDITIONAL INFO:

_____
_____
_____
_____

CLIENT INTAKE

Date: _____

Time frame for selling/buying/renting?
_____

☐ **Buyer**   ☐ **Seller**   ☐ **Renter**   35

First & last name: _____

Contact number: _____ Home/other: _____

Mailing address: _____

Email address: _____

Property of interest: _____ (MLS# _____)

If buying, are you pre-approved? _____ If, yes, with whom? _____

Lead source:

☐ Social media   ☐ Craigslist

☐ Website   ☐ Billboard sign

☐ Newspaper/magazine AD   ☐ Real estate review book

☐ Referref by client | past client | family | friend: _____

What type of property are interested in?

☐ LAND/LOTS/ACERAGE   ☐ RESIDENTIAL   ☐ COMMERCIAL   ☐ INVESTMENT

type of land? acres? aprovements? water? sewer? electric?   sq ft # of beds/ baths acres?   type of building? sq ft? how many rooms? improvements?   type of property? single or multi family home? duplex? 4-plex?

_____

_____

_____

_____

ANY ADDITIONAL INFO:

_____

_____

_____

CLIENT INTAKE

Date: _____

Time frame for selling/buying/renting?
_____

☐ **Buyer**   ☐ **Seller**   ☐ **Renter**   36

First & last name: _____

Contact number: _____ Home/other: _____

Mailing address: _____

Email address: _____

Property of interest: _____ (MLS#   )

If buying, are you pre-approved? _____ If, yes, with whom? _____

Lead source:
☐ Social media   ☐ Craigslist

☐ Website   ☐ Billboard sign

☐ Newspaper/magazine AD   ☐ Real estate review book

☐ Referref by client | past client | family | friend: _____

What type of property are interested in?

☐ LAND/LOTS/ACERAGE   ☐ RESIDENTIAL   ☐ COMMERCIAL   ☐ INVESTMENT

type of land? acres? aprovements? water? sewer? electric?   *sq ft # of beds/ baths acres?*   *type of building? sq ft? how many rooms? improvements?*   *type of property? single or multi family home? duplex? 4-plex?*

_____

_____

_____

_____

ANY ADDITIONAL INFO:

_____

_____

_____

_____

CLIENT INTAKE

Date: _____

Time frame for selling/buying/renting?
_____

☐ **Buyer**　　　☐ **Seller**　　　☐ **Renter**　　　37

First & last name: _____

Contact number: _____ Home/other: _____

Mailing address: _____

Email address: _____

Property of interest: _____ (MLS# _____)

If buying, are you pre-approved? _____ If, yes, with whom? _____

Lead source:
☐ Social media　　　　　　☐ Craigslist

☐ Website　　　　　　　　☐ Billboard sign

☐ Newspaper/magazine AD　☐ Real estate review book

☐ Referref by client | past client | family | friend: _____

What type of property are interested in?

☐ LAND/LOTS/ACERAGE　　☐ RESIDENTIAL　　☐ COMMERCIAL　　☐ INVESTMENT

type of land? acres? aprovements? water? sewer? electric?　　sq ft # of beds/ baths acres?　　type of building? sq ft? how many rooms? improvements?　　type of property? single or multi family home? duplex? 4-plex?

_____

_____

_____

_____

ANY ADDITIONAL INFO:

_____

_____

_____

_____

CLIENT INTAKE

Date: _____

Time frame for selling/buying/renting?

_____

☐ **Buyer**　　　☐ **Seller**　　　☐ **Renter**　　　38

First & last name: _____

Contact number: _____ Home/other: _____

Mailing address: _____

Email address: _____

Property of interest: _____ (MLS#_____)

If buying, are you pre-approved? _____ If, yes, with whom? _____

Lead source:　☐ Social media　　　　　☐ Craigslist

☐ Website　　　　　☐ Billboard sign

☐ Newspaper/magazine AD　　☐ Real estate review book

☐ Referref by client | past client | family | friend: _____

What type of property are interested in?

☐ LAND/LOTS/ACERAGE　☐ RESIDENTIAL　☐ COMMERCIAL　☐ INVESTMENT

type of land? acres? aprovements? water? sewer? electric?　*sq ft # of beds/ baths acres?*　*type of building? sq ft? how many rooms? improvements?*　*type of property? single or multi family home? duplex? 4-plex?*

_____

_____

_____

_____

ANY ADDITIONAL INFO:

_____

_____

_____

_____

CLIENT INTAKE

Date: _____

Time frame for selling/buying/renting?

_____

☐ **Buyer**   ☐ **Seller**   ☐ **Renter**   39

First & last name: _____

Contact number: _____ Home/other: _____

Mailing address: _____

Email address: _____

Property of interest: _____ (MLS#_____)

If buying, are you pre-approved? _____ If, yes, with whom? _____

Lead source: ☐ Social media   ☐ Craigslist

☐ Website   ☐ Billboard sign

☐ Newspaper/magazine AD   ☐ Real estate review book

☐ Referref by client | past client | family | friend: _____

What type of property are interested in?

☐ LAND/LOTS/ACERAGE   ☐ RESIDENTIAL   ☐ COMMERCIAL   ☐ INVESTMENT

type of land? acres? aprovements? water? sewer? electric?   *sq ft # of beds/ baths acres?*   *type of building? sq ft? how many rooms? improvements?*   *type of property? single or multi family home? duplex? 4-plex?*

_____

_____

_____

_____

ANY ADDITIONAL INFO:

_____

_____

_____

_____

CLIENT INTAKE

Date: _____

Time frame for selling/buying/renting?
_____

☐ **Buyer**   ☐ **Seller**   ☐ **Renter**   40

First & last name: _____

Contact number: _____ Home/other: _____

Mailing address: _____

Email address: _____

Property of interest: _____ (MLS# _____)

If buying, are you pre-approved? _____ If, yes, with whom? _____

Lead source:
☐ Social media   ☐ Craigslist

☐ Website   ☐ Billboard sign

☐ Newspaper/magazine AD   ☐ Real estate review book

☐ Referref by client | past client | family | friend: _____

What type of property are interested in?

☐ LAND/LOTS/ACERAGE   ☐ RESIDENTIAL   ☐ COMMERCIAL   ☐ INVESTMENT

type of land? acres? aprovements? water? sewer? electric?   *sq ft # of beds/ baths acres?*   *type of building? sq ft? how many rooms? improvements?*   *type of property? single or multi family home? duplex? 4-plex?*

_____

_____

_____

_____

ANY ADDITIONAL INFO:

_____

_____

_____

_____

CLIENT INTAKE

Date: _____

Time frame for selling/buying/renting?

_____

☐ **Buyer**   ☐ **Seller**   ☐ **Renter**   41

First & last name: _____

Contact number: _____ Home/other: _____

Mailing address: _____

Email address: _____

Property of interest: _____ (MLS#   )

If buying, are you pre-approved? _____ If, yes, with whom? _____

Lead source: ☐ Social media   ☐ Craigslist

☐ Website   ☐ Billboard sign

☐ Newspaper/magazine AD   ☐ Real estate review book

☐ Referref by client | past client | family | friend: _____

What type of property are interested in?

☐ LAND/LOTS/ACERAGE   ☐ RESIDENTIAL   ☐ COMMERCIAL   ☐ INVESTMENT

type of land? acres? aprovements?   sq ft # of beds/ baths acres?   type of building? sq ft?   type of property? single or multi
water? sewer? electric?   how many rooms? improvements?   family home? duplex? 4-plex?

_____

_____

_____

_____

ANY ADDITIONAL INFO:

_____

_____

_____

_____

CLIENT INTAKE

Date: _____

Time frame for selling/buying/renting?
_____

☐ *Buyer*   ☐ *Seller*   ☐ *Renter*   42

First & last name: _____

Contact number: _____ Home/other: _____

Mailing address: _____

Email address: _____

Property of interest: _____ (MLS# _____)

If buying, are you pre-approved? _____ If, yes, with whom? _____

Lead source:
☐ Social media   ☐ Craigslist

☐ Website   ☐ Billboard sign

☐ Newspaper/magazine AD   ☐ Real estate review book

☐ Referref by client | past client | family | friend: _____

What type of property are interested in?

☐ LAND/LOTS/ACERAGE   ☐ RESIDENTIAL   ☐ COMMERCIAL   ☐ INVESTMENT

type of land? acres? aprovements? water? sewer? electric? | *sq ft # of beds/ baths acres?* | *type of building? sq ft? how many rooms? improvements?* | *type of property? single or multi family home? duplex? 4-plex?*

_____

_____

_____

_____

ANY ADDITIONAL INFO:

_____

_____

_____

_____

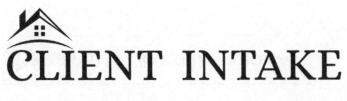

CLIENT INTAKE

Date: _____

Time frame for selling/buying/renting?

_____

☐ **Buyer**   ☐ **Seller**   ☐ **Renter**   43

First & last name: _____

Contact number: _____ Home/other: _____

Mailing address: _____

Email address: _____

Property of interest: _____ (MLS# ____)

If buying, are you pre-approved? _____ If, yes, with whom? _____

Lead source:

☐ Social media   ☐ Craigslist

☐ Website   ☐ Billboard sign

☐ Newspaper/magazine AD ☐ Real estate review book

☐ Referref by client | past client | family | friend: _____

What type of property are interested in?

☐ LAND/LOTS/ACERAGE
type of land? acres? aprovements? water? sewer? electric?

☐ RESIDENTIAL
sq ft # of beds/ baths acres?

☐ COMMERCIAL
type of building? sq ft? how many rooms? improvements?

☐ INVESTMENT
type of property? single or multi family home? duplex? 4-plex?

_____

_____

_____

_____

ANY ADDITIONAL INFO:

_____

_____

_____

_____

CLIENT INTAKE

Date: _____

Time frame for selling/buying/renting?
_____

☐ **Buyer**　　　☐ **Seller**　　　☐ **Renter**　　　44

First & last name: _____

Contact number: _____ Home/other: _____

Mailing address: _____

Email address: _____

Property of interest: _____ (MLS# _____)

If buying, are you pre-approved? _____ If, yes, with whom? _____

Lead source:　☐ Social media　　　　☐ Craigslist

☐ Website　　　　☐ Billboard sign

☐ Newspaper/magazine AD　☐ Real estate review book

☐ Referref by client | past client | family | friend: _____

What type of property are interested in?

☐ LAND/LOTS/ACERAGE　☐ RESIDENTIAL　☐ COMMERCIAL　☐ INVESTMENT

type of land? acres? aprovements? water? sewer? electric?　　sq ft # of beds/ baths acres?　　type of building? sq ft? how many rooms? improvements?　　type of property? single or multi family home? duplex? 4-plex?

_____

_____

_____

_____

ANY ADDITIONAL INFO:

_____

_____

_____

CLIENT INTAKE

Date: _____

Time frame for selling/buying/renting?
_____

☐ **Buyer**   ☐ **Seller**   ☐ **Renter**   45

First & last name: _____

Contact number: _____ Home/other: _____

Mailing address: _____

Email address: _____

Property of interest: _____ (MLS#   )

If buying, are you pre-approved? _____ If, yes, with whom? _____

Lead source: ☐ Social media   ☐ Craigslist

☐ Website   ☐ Billboard sign

☐ Newspaper/magazine AD   ☐ Real estate review book

☐ Referref by client | past client | family | friend: _____

What type of property are interested in?

☐ LAND/LOTS/ACERAGE   ☐ RESIDENTIAL   ☐ COMMERCIAL   ☐ INVESTMENT

type of land? acres? aprovements?   sq ft # of beds/ baths acres?   type of building? sq ft?   type of property? single or multi
water? sewer? electric?   how many rooms? improvements?   family home? duplex? 4-plex?

_____

_____

_____

_____

ANY ADDITIONAL INFO:

_____

_____

_____

_____

CLIENT INTAKE

Date: _____

Time frame for selling/buying/renting?

_____

☐ **Buyer**   ☐ **Seller**   ☐ **Renter**   46

First & last name: _____

Contact number: _____ Home/other: _____

Mailing address: _____

Email address: _____

Property of interest: _____ (MLS#   )

If buying, are you pre-approved? _____ If, yes, with whom? _____

Lead source: ☐ Social media   ☐ Craigslist

☐ Website   ☐ Billboard sign

☐ Newspaper/magazine AD   ☐ Real estate review book

☐ Referref by client | past client | family | friend: _____

What type of property are interested in?

☐ LAND/LOTS/ACERAGE   ☐ RESIDENTIAL   ☐ COMMERCIAL   ☐ INVESTMENT

type of land? acres? aprovements? water? sewer? electric?   *sq ft # of beds/ baths acres?*   *type of building? sq ft? how many rooms? improvements?*   *type of property? single or multi family home? duplex? 4-plex?*

_____

_____

_____

_____

ANY ADDITIONAL INFO:

_____

_____

_____

_____

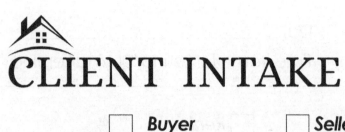

CLIENT INTAKE

Date: _____

Time frame for selling/buying/renting?

_____

☐ **Buyer**   ☐ **Seller**   ☐ **Renter**   47

First & last name: _____

Contact number: _____ Home/other: _____

Mailing address: _____

Email address: _____

Property of interest: _____ (MLS# ____)

If buying, are you pre-approved? _____ If, yes, with whom? _____

Lead source:

☐ Social media   ☐ Craigslist

☐ Website   ☐ Billboard sign

☐ Newspaper/magazine AD   ☐ Real estate review book

☐ Referref by client | past client | family | friend: _____

What type of property are interested in?

☐ LAND/LOTS/ACERAGE   ☐ RESIDENTIAL   ☐ COMMERCIAL   ☐ INVESTMENT

type of land? acres? aprovements? | sq ft # of beds/ baths acres? | type of building? sq ft? how many rooms? improvements? | type of property? single or multi family home? duplex? 4-plex?
water? sewer? electric?

_____

_____

_____

_____

ANY ADDITIONAL INFO:

_____

_____

_____

_____

CLIENT INTAKE

Date: _____

Time frame for selling/buying/renting?

_____

☐ **Buyer**　　　☐ **Seller**　　　☐ **Renter**　　48

First & last name: _____

Contact number: _____ Home/other: _____

Mailing address: _____

Email address: _____

Property of interest: _____ (MLS#　　　　)

If buying, are you pre-approved? _____ If, yes, with whom? _____

Lead source:　☐ Social media　　　　☐ Craigslist

☐ Website　　　　☐ Billboard sign

☐ Newspaper/magazine AD　　☐ Real estate review book

☐ Referref by client | past client | family | friend: _____

What type of property are interested in?

☐ LAND/LOTS/ACERAGE　　☐ RESIDENTIAL　　☐ COMMERCIAL　　☐ INVESTMENT

type of land? acres? aprovements? water? sewer? electric?　　*sq ft # of beds/ baths acres?*　　*type of building? sq ft? how many rooms? improvements?*　　*type of property? single or multi family home? duplex? 4-plex?*

_____

_____

_____

_____

ANY ADDITIONAL INFO:

_____

_____

_____

_____

CLIENT INTAKE

Date: _____

Time frame for selling/buying/renting?
_____

☐ **Buyer**   ☐ **Seller**   ☐ **Renter**   49

First & last name: _____

Contact number: _____ Home/other: _____

Mailing address: _____

Email address: _____

Property of interest: _____ (MLS# _____)

If buying, are you pre-approved? _____ If, yes, with whom? _____

Lead source:
☐ Social media   ☐ Craigslist

☐ Website   ☐ Billboard sign

☐ Newspaper/magazine AD   ☐ Real estate review book

☐ Referref by client | past client | family | friend: _____

What type of property are interested in?

☐ LAND/LOTS/ACERAGE   ☐ RESIDENTIAL   ☐ COMMERCIAL   ☐ INVESTMENT

type of land? acres? aprovements?   sq ft # of beds/ baths acres?   type of building? sq ft?   type of property? single or multi
water? sewer? electric?   how many rooms? improvements?   family home? duplex? 4-plex?

_____

_____

_____

_____

ANY ADDITIONAL INFO:

_____

_____

_____

_____

CLIENT INTAKE

Date: _____

Time frame for selling/buying/renting?
_____

☐ **Buyer**   ☐ **Seller**   ☐ **Renter**   50

First & last name: _____

Contact number: _____ Home/other: _____

Mailing address: _____

Email address: _____

Property of interest: _____ (MLS# ____)

If buying, are you pre-approved? _____ If, yes, with whom? _____

Lead source: ☐ Social media   ☐ Craigslist

☐ Website   ☐ Billboard sign

☐ Newspaper/magazine AD   ☐ Real estate review book

☐ Referref by client | past client | family | friend: _____

What type of property are interested in?

☐ LAND/LOTS/ACERAGE   ☐ RESIDENTIAL   ☐ COMMERCIAL   ☐ INVESTMENT

type of land? acres? aprovements? water? sewer? electric?   sq ft # of beds/ baths acres?   type of building? sq ft? how many rooms? improvements?   type of property? single or multi family home? duplex? 4-plex?

_____

_____

_____

_____

ANY ADDITIONAL INFO:

_____

_____

_____

_____

CLIENT INTAKE

Date: _____

Time frame for selling/buying/renting?
_____

☐ **Buyer**   ☐ **Seller**   ☐ **Renter**   51

First & last name: _____

Contact number: _____ Home/other: _____

Mailing address: _____

Email address: _____

Property of interest: _____ (MLS# _____)

If buying, are you pre-approved? _____ If, yes, with whom? _____

Lead source:
☐ Social media   ☐ Craigslist

☐ Website   ☐ Billboard sign

☐ Newspaper/magazine AD   ☐ Real estate review book

☐ Referref by client | past client | family | friend: _____

What type of property are interested in?

☐ *LAND/LOTS/ACERAGE*   ☐ *RESIDENTIAL*   ☐ *COMMERCIAL*   ☐ *INVESTMENT*

type of land? acres? aprovements? water? sewer? electric?   *sq ft # of beds/ baths acres?*   *type of building? sq ft? how many rooms? improvements?*   *type of property? single or multi family home? duplex? 4-plex?*

_____

_____

_____

_____

ANY ADDITIONAL INFO:

_____

_____

_____

_____

CLIENT INTAKE

Date: _____

Time frame for selling/buying/renting?
_____

☐ **Buyer**   ☐ **Seller**   ☐ **Renter**   52

First & last name: _____

Contact number: _____ Home/other: _____

Mailing address: _____

Email address: _____

Property of interest: _____ (MLS#   )

If buying, are you pre-approved? _____ If, yes, with whom? _____

Lead source:
☐ Social media   ☐ Craigslist

☐ Website   ☐ Billboard sign

☐ Newspaper/magazine AD   ☐ Real estate review book

☐ Referref by client | past client | family | friend: _____

What type of property are interested in?

☐ LAND/LOTS/ACERAGE   ☐ RESIDENTIAL   ☐ COMMERCIAL   ☐ INVESTMENT

type of land? acres? aprovements? water? sewer? electric?   *sq ft # of beds/ baths acres?*   *type of building? sq ft? how many rooms? improvements?*   *type of property? single or multi family home? duplex? 4-plex?*

_____

_____

_____

_____

ANY ADDITIONAL INFO:

_____

_____

_____

_____

CLIENT INTAKE

Date: _____

Time frame for selling/buying/renting?

_____

☐ **Buyer**   ☐ **Seller**   ☐ **Renter**   53

First & last name: _____

Contact number: _____ Home/other: _____

Mailing address: _____

Email address: _____

Property of interest: _____ (MLS#   )

If buying, are you pre-approved? _____ If, yes, with whom? _____

Lead source: ☐ Social media   ☐ Craigslist

☐ Website   ☐ Billboard sign

☐ Newspaper/magazine AD   ☐ Real estate review book

☐ Referref by client | past client | family | friend: _____

What type of property are interested in?

☐ LAND/LOTS/ACERAGE   ☐ RESIDENTIAL   ☐ COMMERCIAL   ☐ INVESTMENT

type of land? acres? aprovements?   sq ft # of beds/ baths acres?   type of building? sq ft?   type of property? single or multi
water? sewer? electric?   how many rooms? improvements?   family home? duplex? 4-plex?

_____

_____

_____

_____

ANY ADDITIONAL INFO:

_____

_____

_____

_____

CLIENT INTAKE

Date: _____

Time frame for selling/buying/renting?

_____

☐ **Buyer**   ☐ **Seller**   ☐ **Renter**   54

First & last name: _____

Contact number: _____ Home/other: _____

Mailing address: _____

Email address: _____

Property of interest: _____ (MLS# ____)

If buying, are you pre-approved? _____ If, yes, with whom? _____

Lead source:
☐ Social media   ☐ Craigslist

☐ Website   ☐ Billboard sign

☐ Newspaper/magazine AD ☐ Real estate review book

☐ Referref by client | past client | family | friend: _____

What type of property are interested in?

☐ LAND/LOTS/ACERAGE   ☐ RESIDENTIAL   ☐ COMMERCIAL   ☐ INVESTMENT

type of land? acres? aprovements? water? sewer? electric? | *sq ft # of beds/ baths acres?* | *type of building? sq ft? how many rooms? improvements?* | *type of property? single or multi family home? duplex? 4-plex?*

_____

_____

_____

_____

ANY ADDITIONAL INFO:

_____

_____

_____

_____

CLIENT INTAKE

Date: _____

Time frame for selling/buying/renting?
_____

☐ **Buyer**　　　☐ **Seller**　　　☐ **Renter**　　　55

First & last name: _____

Contact number: _____ Home/other: _____

Mailing address: _____

Email address: _____

Property of interest: _____ (MLS#　　　)

If buying, are you pre-approved? _____ If, yes, with whom? _____

Lead source:　☐ Social media　　　　☐ Craigslist

　　　　　　　☐ Website　　　　　　☐ Billboard sign

　　　　　　　☐ Newspaper/magazine AD　☐ Real estate review book

　　　　　　　☐ Referref by client | past client | family | friend: _____

What type of property are interested in?

☐ LAND/LOTS/ACERAGE　☐ RESIDENTIAL　☐ COMMERCIAL　☐ INVESTMENT

type of land? acres? aprovements? water? sewer? electric? | *sq ft # of beds/ baths acres?* | *type of building? sq ft? how many rooms? improvements?* | *type of property? single or multi family home? duplex? 4-plex?*

_____

_____

_____

_____

ANY ADDITIONAL INFO:

_____

_____

_____

CLIENT INTAKE

Date: _____

Time frame for selling/buying/renting?
_____

☐ **Buyer**　　　☐ **Seller**　　　☐ **Renter**　　　56

First & last name: _____

Contact number: _____ Home/other: _____

Mailing address: _____

Email address: _____

Property of interest: _____ (MLS#　　　)

If buying, are you pre-approved? _____ If, yes, with whom? _____

Lead source:
☐ Social media　　　　　　　☐ Craigslist

☐ Website　　　　　　　　　☐ Billboard sign

☐ Newspaper/magazine AD　　☐ Real estate review book

☐ Referref by client | past client | family | friend: _____

What type of property are interested in?

☐ LAND/LOTS/ACERAGE　☐ RESIDENTIAL　☐ COMMERCIAL　☐ INVESTMENT

type of land? acres? aprovements? water? sewer? electric?　*sq ft # of beds/ baths acres?*　*type of building? sq ft? how many rooms? improvements?*　*type of property? single or multi family home? duplex? 4-plex?*

_____

_____

_____

_____

ANY ADDITIONAL INFO:

_____

_____

_____

_____

CLIENT INTAKE

Date: _____

Time frame for selling/buying/renting?
_____

☐ **Buyer**   ☐ **Seller**   ☐ **Renter**   57

First & last name: _____

Contact number: _____ Home/other: _____

Mailing address: _____

Email address: _____

Property of interest: _____ (MLS# _____)

If buying, are you pre-approved? _____ If, yes, with whom? _____

Lead source: ☐ Social media   ☐ Craigslist

☐ Website   ☐ Billboard sign

☐ Newspaper/magazine AD   ☐ Real estate review book

☐ Referref by client | past client | family | friend: _____

What type of property are interested in?

☐ LAND/LOTS/ACERAGE   ☐ RESIDENTIAL   ☐ COMMERCIAL   ☐ INVESTMENT

type of land? acres? aprovements?   sq ft # of beds/ baths acres?   type of building? sq ft?   type of property? single or multi
water? sewer? electric?   how many rooms? improvements?   family home? duplex? 4-plex?

_____

_____

_____

_____

ANY ADDITIONAL INFO:

_____

_____

_____

_____

CLIENT INTAKE

Date: _____

Time frame for selling/buying/renting?
_____

☐ **Buyer**　　　☐ **Seller**　　　☐ **Renter**　　　58

First & last name: _____

Contact number: _____ Home/other: _____

Mailing address: _____

Email address: _____

Property of interest: _____ (MLS# _____)

If buying, are you pre-approved? _____ If, yes, with whom? _____

Lead source:
☐ Social media　　　　　☐ Craigslist

☐ Website　　　　　　　☐ Billboard sign

☐ Newspaper/magazine AD　☐ Real estate review book

☐ Referref by client | past client | family | friend: _____

What type of property are interested in?

☐ LAND/LOTS/ACERAGE　☐ RESIDENTIAL　☐ COMMERCIAL　☐ INVESTMENT

type of land? acres? aprovements? water? sewer? electric?　sq ft # of beds/ baths acres?　type of building? sq ft? how many rooms? improvements?　type of property? single or multi family home? duplex? 4-plex?

_____

_____

_____

_____

ANY ADDITIONAL INFO:

_____

_____

_____

_____

CLIENT INTAKE

Date: _____

Time frame for selling/buying/renting?

_____

☐ **Buyer**   ☐ **Seller**   ☐ **Renter**   59

First & last name: _____

Contact number: _____ Home/other: _____

Mailing address: _____

Email address: _____

Property of interest: _____ (MLS#   )

If buying, are you pre-approved? _____ If, yes, with whom? _____

Lead source: ☐ Social media   ☐ Craigslist

☐ Website   ☐ Billboard sign

☐ Newspaper/magazine AD   ☐ Real estate review book

☐ Referref by client | past client | family | friend: _____

What type of property are interested in?

☐ LAND/LOTS/ACERAGE   ☐ RESIDENTIAL   ☐ COMMERCIAL   ☐ INVESTMENT

type of land? acres? aprovements?   sq ft # of beds/ baths acres?   type of building? sq ft?   type of property? single or multi
water? sewer? electric?   how many rooms? improvements?   family home? duplex? 4-plex?

_____

_____

_____

_____

ANY ADDITIONAL INFO:

_____

_____

_____

_____

CLIENT INTAKE

Date: _____

Time frame for selling/buying/renting?
_____

☐ **Buyer**　　　　☐ **Seller**　　　　☐ **Renter**　　　60

First & last name: _____

Contact number: _____ Home/other: _____

Mailing address: _____

Email address: _____

Property of interest: _____ (MLS#　　　　)

If buying, are you pre-approved? _____ If, yes, with whom? _____

Lead source:
☐ Social media　　　　　　☐ Craigslist

☐ Website　　　　　　　　☐ Billboard sign

☐ Newspaper/magazine AD　☐ Real estate review book

☐ Referref by client | past client | family | friend: _____

What type of property are interested in?

☐ LAND/LOTS/ACERAGE　　☐ RESIDENTIAL　　☐ COMMERCIAL　　☐ INVESTMENT

type of land? acres? aprovements?　sq ft # of beds/ baths acres?　type of building? sq ft?　type of property? single or multi
water? sewer? electric?　　　　　　　　　　　　　　　　how many rooms? improvements?　family home? duplex? 4-plex?

_____

_____

_____

_____

ANY ADDITIONAL INFO:

_____

_____

_____

_____

CLIENT INTAKE

Date: _____

Time frame for selling/buying/renting?
_____

☐ **Buyer**   ☐ **Seller**   ☐ **Renter**   61

First & last name: _____

Contact number: _____ Home/other: _____

Mailing address: _____

Email address: _____

Property of interest: _____ (MLS# _____)

If buying, are you pre-approved? _____ If, yes, with whom? _____

Lead source: ☐ Social media   ☐ Craigslist

☐ Website   ☐ Billboard sign

☐ Newspaper/magazine AD   ☐ Real estate review book

☐ Referref by client | past client | family | friend: _____

What type of property are interested in?

☐ LAND/LOTS/ACERAGE   ☐ RESIDENTIAL   ☐ COMMERCIAL   ☐ INVESTMENT

type of land? acres? aprovements? water? sewer? electric?   sq ft # of beds/ baths acres?   type of building? sq ft? how many rooms? improvements?   type of property? single or multi family home? duplex? 4-plex?

_____

_____

_____

_____

ANY ADDITIONAL INFO:

_____

_____

_____

_____

CLIENT INTAKE

Date: _____

Time frame for selling/buying/renting?
_____

☐ **Buyer**   ☐ **Seller**   ☐ **Renter**   62

First & last name: _____

Contact number: _____ Home/other: _____

Mailing address: _____

Email address: _____

Property of interest: _____ (MLS# _____)

If buying, are you pre-approved? _____ If, yes, with whom? _____

Lead source:
☐ Social media   ☐ Craigslist

☐ Website   ☐ Billboard sign

☐ Newspaper/magazine AD   ☐ Real estate review book

☐ Referref by client | past client | family | friend: _____

What type of property are interested in?

☐ LAND/LOTS/ACERAGE	☐ RESIDENTIAL	☐ COMMERCIAL	☐ INVESTMENT
type of land? acres? aprovements? water? sewer? electric?	sq ft # of beds/ baths acres?	type of building? sq ft? how many rooms? improvements?	type of property? single or multi family home? duplex? 4-plex?

_____

_____

_____

_____

ANY ADDITIONAL INFO:

_____

_____

_____

_____

CLIENT INTAKE

Date: _____

Time frame for selling/buying/renting?

_____

☐ **Buyer**　　　☐ **Seller**　　　☐ **Renter**　　　63

First & last name: _____

Contact number: _____ Home/other: _____

Mailing address: _____

Email address: _____

Property of interest: _____ (MLS# _____)

If buying, are you pre-approved? _____ If, yes, with whom? _____

Lead source:　☐ Social media　　　　　☐ Craigslist

　　　　　　　　☐ Website　　　　　　　☐ Billboard sign

　　　　　　　　☐ Newspaper/magazine AD　☐ Real estate review book

　　　　　　　　☐ Referref by client | past client | family | friend: _____

What type of property are interested in?

☐ LAND/LOTS/ACERAGE　☐ RESIDENTIAL　☐ COMMERCIAL　☐ INVESTMENT

type of land? acres? aprovements? water? sewer? electric?　sq ft # of beds/ baths acres?　type of building? sq ft? how many rooms? improvements?　type of property? single or multi family home? duplex? 4-plex?

_____

_____

_____

_____

ANY ADDITIONAL INFO:

_____

_____

_____

_____

CLIENT INTAKE

Date: _____

Time frame for selling/buying/renting?

_____

☐ **Buyer**   ☐ **Seller**   ☐ **Renter**   64

First & last name: _____

Contact number: _____ Home/other: _____

Mailing address: _____

Email address: _____

Property of interest: _____ (MLS#   )

If buying, are you pre-approved? _____ If, yes, with whom? _____

Lead source: ☐ Social media   ☐ Craigslist

☐ Website   ☐ Billboard sign

☐ Newspaper/magazine AD   ☐ Real estate review book

☐ Referref by client | past client | family | friend: _____

What type of property are interested in?

☐ LAND/LOTS/ACERAGE   ☐ RESIDENTIAL   ☐ COMMERCIAL   ☐ INVESTMENT

type of land? acres? aprovements? water? sewer? electric? / sq ft # of beds/ baths acres? / type of building? sq ft? how many rooms? improvements? / type of property? single or multi family home? duplex? 4-plex?

_____

_____

_____

_____

ANY ADDITIONAL INFO:

_____

_____

_____

_____

CLIENT INTAKE

Date: _____

Time frame for selling/buying/renting?

_____

☐ **Buyer**　　　☐ **Seller**　　　☐ **Renter**　　65

First & last name: _____

Contact number: _____ Home/other: _____

Mailing address: _____

Email address: _____

Property of interest: _____ (MLS#　　　　)

If buying, are you pre-approved? _____ If, yes, with whom? _____

Lead source:　☐ Social media　　　　　☐ Craigslist

　　　　　　　☐ Website　　　　　　　☐ Billboard sign

　　　　　　　☐ Newspaper/magazine AD　☐ Real estate review book

　　　　　　　☐ Referref by client | past client | family | friend: _____

What type of property are interested in?

☐ LAND/LOTS/ACERAGE　☐ RESIDENTIAL　☐ COMMERCIAL　☐ INVESTMENT

type of land? acres? aprovements? water? sewer? electric?　　sq ft # of beds/ baths acres?　　type of building? sq ft? how many rooms? improvements?　　type of property? single or multi family home? duplex? 4-plex?

_____

_____

_____

ANY ADDITIONAL INFO:

_____

_____

_____

CLIENT INTAKE

Date: _____

Time frame for selling/buying/renting?

_____

☐ **Buyer**   ☐ **Seller**   ☐ **Renter**   66

First & last name: _____

Contact number: _____ Home/other: _____

Mailing address: _____

Email address: _____

Property of interest: _____ (MLS# ____)

If buying, are you pre-approved? _____ If, yes, with whom? _____

Lead source: ☐ Social media   ☐ Craigslist

☐ Website   ☐ Billboard sign

☐ Newspaper/magazine AD   ☐ Real estate review book

☐ Referref by client | past client | family | friend: _____

What type of property are interested in?

☐ LAND/LOTS/ACERAGE   ☐ RESIDENTIAL   ☐ COMMERCIAL   ☐ INVESTMENT

type of land? acres? aprovements? water? sewer? electric? | sq ft # of beds/ baths acres? | type of building? sq ft? how many rooms? improvements? | type of property? single or multi family home? duplex? 4-plex?

_____

_____

_____

_____

ANY ADDITIONAL INFO:

_____

_____

_____

_____

CLIENT INTAKE

Date: _____

Time frame for selling/buying/renting?
_____

☐ **Buyer**　　☐ **Seller**　　☐ **Renter**　　67

First & last name: _____

Contact number: _____ Home/other: _____

Mailing address: _____

Email address: _____

Property of interest: _____ (MLS# _____)

If buying, are you pre-approved? _____ If, yes, with whom? _____

Lead source:　
☐ Social media　　　　　☐ Craigslist

☐ Website　　　　　　　☐ Billboard sign

☐ Newspaper/magazine AD　☐ Real estate review book

☐ Referref by client | past client | family | friend: _____

What type of property are interested in?

☐ LAND/LOTS/ACERAGE　　☐ RESIDENTIAL　　☐ COMMERCIAL　　☐ INVESTMENT

type of land? acres? aprovements? water? sewer? electric?　
sq ft # of beds/ baths acres?　
type of building? sq ft? how many rooms? improvements?　
type of property? single or multi family home? duplex? 4-plex?

_____

_____

_____

_____

ANY ADDITIONAL INFO:

_____

_____

_____

_____

CLIENT INTAKE

Date: _____

Time frame for selling/buying/renting?

_____

☐ **Buyer**   ☐ **Seller**   ☐ **Renter**   68

First & last name: _____

Contact number: _____ Home/other: _____

Mailing address: _____

Email address: _____

Property of interest: _____ (MLS# _____)

If buying, are you pre-approved? _____ If, yes, with whom? _____

Lead source: ☐ Social media   ☐ Craigslist

☐ Website   ☐ Billboard sign

☐ Newspaper/magazine AD   ☐ Real estate review book

☐ Referref by client | past client | family | friend: _____

What type of property are interested in?

☐ LAND/LOTS/ACERAGE   ☐ RESIDENTIAL   ☐ COMMERCIAL   ☐ INVESTMENT

type of land? acres? aprovements?   sq ft # of beds/ baths acres?   type of building? sq ft?   type of property? single or multi
water? sewer? electric?   how many rooms? improvements?   family home? duplex? 4-plex?

_____

_____

_____

_____

ANY ADDITIONAL INFO:

_____

_____

_____

_____

CLIENT INTAKE

Date: _____

Time frame for selling/buying/renting?

_____

☐ **Buyer** ☐ **Seller** ☐ **Renter** 69

First & last name: _____

Contact number: _____ Home/other: _____

Mailing address: _____

Email address: _____

Property of interest: _____ (MLS# ___)

If buying, are you pre-approved? _____ If, yes, with whom? _____

Lead source:
☐ Social media   ☐ Craigslist

☐ Website   ☐ Billboard sign

☐ Newspaper/magazine AD   ☐ Real estate review book

☐ Referref by client | past client | family | friend: _____

What type of property are interested in?

☐ LAND/LOTS/ACERAGE   ☐ RESIDENTIAL   ☐ COMMERCIAL   ☐ INVESTMENT

type of land? acres? aprovements? water? sewer? electric? | sq ft # of beds/ baths acres? | type of building? sq ft? how many rooms? improvements? | type of property? single or multi family home? duplex? 4-plex?

_____

_____

_____

_____

ANY ADDITIONAL INFO:

_____

_____

_____

_____

CLIENT INTAKE

Date: _____

Time frame for selling/buying/renting?
_____

☐ **Buyer**　　☐ **Seller**　　☐ **Renter**　　70

First & last name: _____

Contact number: _____ Home/other: _____

Mailing address: _____

Email address: _____

Property of interest: _____ (MLS# ___)

If buying, are you pre-approved? _____ If, yes, with whom? _____

Lead source:
☐ Social media　　　　☐ Craigslist

☐ Website　　　　　　☐ Billboard sign

☐ Newspaper/magazine AD　☐ Real estate review book

☐ Referref by client | past client | family | friend: _____

What type of property are interested in?

☐ LAND/LOTS/ACERAGE　☐ RESIDENTIAL　☐ COMMERCIAL　☐ INVESTMENT

type of land? acres? aprovements? water? sewer? electric?　*sq ft # of beds/ baths acres?*　*type of building? sq ft? how many rooms? improvements?*　*type of property? single or multi family home? duplex? 4-plex?*

_____

_____

_____

_____

ANY ADDITIONAL INFO:

_____

_____

_____

_____

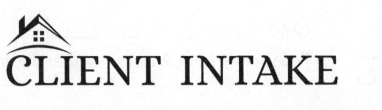

CLIENT INTAKE

Date: _____

Time frame for selling/buying/renting?

_____

☐ **Buyer**   ☐ **Seller**   ☐ **Renter**   71

First & last name: _____

Contact number: _____ Home/other: _____

Mailing address: _____

Email address: _____

Property of interest: _____ (MLS#   )

If buying, are you pre-approved? _____ If, yes, with whom? _____

Lead source: ☐ Social media   ☐ Craigslist

☐ Website   ☐ Billboard sign

☐ Newspaper/magazine AD   ☐ Real estate review book

☐ Referref by client | past client | family | friend: _____

What type of property are interested in?

☐ LAND/LOTS/ACERAGE   ☐ RESIDENTIAL   ☐ COMMERCIAL   ☐ INVESTMENT

type of land? acres? aprovements? water? sewer? electric?   *sq ft # of beds/ baths acres?*   *type of building? sq ft? how many rooms? improvements?*   *type of property? single or multi family home? duplex? 4-plex?*

_____

_____

_____

_____

ANY ADDITIONAL INFO:

_____

_____

_____

_____

CLIENT INTAKE

Date: _____

Time frame for selling/buying/renting?

_____

☐ **Buyer**   ☐ **Seller**   ☐ **Renter**   72

First & last name: _____

Contact number: _____ Home/other: _____

Mailing address: _____

Email address: _____

Property of interest: _____ (MLS#   )

If buying, are you pre-approved? _____ If, yes, with whom? _____

Lead source: ☐ Social media   ☐ Craigslist

                  ☐ Website   ☐ Billboard sign

                  ☐ Newspaper/magazine AD   ☐ Real estate review book

                  ☐ Referref by client | past client | family | friend: _____

What type of property are interested in?

☐ LAND/LOTS/ACERAGE   ☐ RESIDENTIAL   ☐ COMMERCIAL   ☐ INVESTMENT

type of land? acres? aprovements? water? sewer? electric? *sq ft # of beds/ baths acres?* *type of building? sq ft? how many rooms? improvements?* *type of property? single or multi family home? duplex? 4-plex?*

_____

_____

_____

_____

ANY ADDITIONAL INFO:

_____

_____

_____

_____

CLIENT INTAKE

Date: _____

Time frame for selling/buying/renting?
_____

☐ **Buyer**   ☐ **Seller**   ☐ **Renter**   73

First & last name: _____

Contact number: _____ Home/other: _____

Mailing address: _____

Email address: _____

Property of interest: _____ (MLS# _____)

If buying, are you pre-approved? _____ If, yes, with whom? _____

Lead source: ☐ Social media   ☐ Craigslist

☐ Website   ☐ Billboard sign

☐ Newspaper/magazine AD   ☐ Real estate review book

☐ Referref by client | past client | family | friend: _____

What type of property are interested in?

☐ LAND/LOTS/ACERAGE   ☐ RESIDENTIAL   ☐ COMMERCIAL   ☐ INVESTMENT

type of land? acres? aprovements?   sq ft # of beds/ baths acres?   type of building? sq ft?   type of property? single or multi
water? sewer? electric?   how many rooms? improvements?   family home? duplex? 4-plex?

_____

_____

_____

_____

ANY ADDITIONAL INFO:

_____

_____

_____

_____

CLIENT INTAKE

Date: _____

Time frame for selling/buying/renting?

_____

☐ **Buyer**　　　☐ **Seller**　　　☐ **Renter**　　　74

First & last name: _____

Contact number: _____ Home/other: _____

Mailing address: _____

Email address: _____

Property of interest: _____ (MLS# _____)

If buying, are you pre-approved? _____ If, yes, with whom? _____

Lead source:　　☐ Social media　　　　☐ Craigslist

　　　　　　　　　☐ Website　　　　　　☐ Billboard sign

　　　　　　　　　☐ Newspaper/magazine AD　　☐ Real estate review book

　　　　　　　　　☐ Referref by client | past client | family | friend: _____

What type of property are interested in?

☐ LAND/LOTS/ACERAGE　　☐ RESIDENTIAL　　☐ COMMERCIAL　　☐ INVESTMENT

type of land? acres? aprovements?　　sq ft # of beds/ baths acres?　　type of building? sq ft?　　type of property? single or multi
water? sewer? electric?　　　　　　　　　　　　　　　　how many rooms? improvements?　　family home? duplex? 4-plex?

_____

_____

_____

_____

ANY ADDITIONAL INFO:

_____

_____

_____

_____

CLIENT INTAKE

Date: _____

Time frame for selling/buying/renting?
_____

☐ **Buyer**　　　☐ **Seller**　　　☐ **Renter**　　75

First & last name: _____

Contact number: _____ Home/other: _____

Mailing address: _____

Email address: _____

Property of interest: _____ (MLS# _____)

If buying, are you pre-approved? _____ If, yes, with whom? _____

Lead source:
☐ Social media　　　　　　☐ Craigslist

☐ Website　　　　　　　　☐ Billboard sign

☐ Newspaper/magazine AD　☐ Real estate review book

☐ Referref by client | past client | family | friend: _____

What type of property are interested in?

☐ LAND/LOTS/ACERAGE　　☐ RESIDENTIAL　　☐ COMMERCIAL　　☐ INVESTMENT

type of land? acres? aprovements? water? sewer? electric?　*sq ft # of beds/ baths acres?*　*type of building? sq ft? how many rooms? improvements?*　*type of property? single or multi family home? duplex? 4-plex?*

_____

_____

_____

_____

ANY ADDITIONAL INFO:

_____

_____

_____

_____

CLIENT INTAKE

Date: _____

Time frame for selling/buying/renting?
_____

☐ **Buyer**   ☐ **Seller**   ☐ **Renter**   76

First & last name: _____

Contact number: _____ Home/other: _____

Mailing address: _____

Email address: _____

Property of interest: _____ (MLS#   )

If buying, are you pre-approved? _____ If, yes, with whom? _____

Lead source: ☐ Social media   ☐ Craigslist

☐ Website   ☐ Billboard sign

☐ Newspaper/magazine AD   ☐ Real estate review book

☐ Referref by client | past client | family | friend: _____

What type of property are interested in?

☐ LAND/LOTS/ACERAGE   ☐ RESIDENTIAL   ☐ COMMERCIAL   ☐ INVESTMENT

type of land? acres? aprovements? water? sewer? electric?   *sq ft # of beds/ baths acres?*   *type of building? sq ft? how many rooms? improvements?*   *type of property? single or multi family home? duplex? 4-plex?*

_____

_____

_____

_____

ANY ADDITIONAL INFO:

_____

_____

_____

_____

CLIENT INTAKE

Date: _____

Time frame for selling/buying/renting?

_____

☐ **Buyer**   ☐ **Seller**   ☐ **Renter**   77

First & last name: _____

Contact number: _____ Home/other: _____

Mailing address: _____

Email address: _____

Property of interest: _____ (MLS# _____)

If buying, are you pre-approved? _____ If, yes, with whom? _____

Lead source: ☐ Social media   ☐ Craigslist

☐ Website   ☐ Billboard sign

☐ Newspaper/magazine AD   ☐ Real estate review book

☐ Referref by client | past client | family | friend: _____

What type of property are interested in?

☐ LAND/LOTS/ACERAGE   ☐ RESIDENTIAL   ☐ COMMERCIAL   ☐ INVESTMENT

type of land? acres? aprovements? water? sewer? electric?   *sq ft # of beds/ baths acres?*   *type of building? sq ft? how many rooms? improvements?*   *type of property? single or multi family home? duplex? 4-plex?*

_____

_____

_____

_____

ANY ADDITIONAL INFO:

_____

_____

_____

_____

CLIENT INTAKE

Date: _____

Time frame for selling/buying/renting?

_____

☐ **Buyer**   ☐ **Seller**   ☐ **Renter**   78

First & last name: _____

Contact number: _____ Home/other: _____

Mailing address: _____

Email address: _____

Property of interest: _____ (MLS# _____)

If buying, are you pre-approved? _____ If, yes, with whom? _____

Lead source:
☐ Social media   ☐ Craigslist

☐ Website   ☐ Billboard sign

☐ Newspaper/magazine AD   ☐ Real estate review book

☐ Referref by client | past client | family | friend: _____

What type of property are interested in?

☐ LAND/LOTS/ACERAGE
type of land? acres? aprovements?
water? sewer? electric?

☐ RESIDENTIAL
sq ft # of beds/ baths acres?

☐ COMMERCIAL
type of building? sq ft?
how many rooms? improvements?

☐ INVESTMENT
type of property? single or multi
family home? duplex? 4-plex?

_____

_____

_____

_____

ANY ADDITIONAL INFO:

_____

_____

_____

_____

CLIENT INTAKE

Date: _____

Time frame for selling/buying/renting?

_____

☐ **Buyer**   ☐ **Seller**   ☐ **Renter**   79

First & last name: _____

Contact number: _____ Home/other: _____

Mailing address: _____

Email address: _____

Property of interest: _____ (MLS#   )

If buying, are you pre-approved? _____ If, yes, with whom? _____

Lead source: ☐ Social media   ☐ Craigslist

☐ Website   ☐ Billboard sign

☐ Newspaper/magazine AD   ☐ Real estate review book

☐ Referref by client | past client | family | friend: _____

What type of property are interested in?

☐ LAND/LOTS/ACERAGE   ☐ RESIDENTIAL   ☐ COMMERCIAL   ☐ INVESTMENT

type of land? acres? aprovements? water? sewer? electric?   *sq ft # of beds/ baths acres?*   *type of building? sq ft? how many rooms? improvements?*   *type of property? single or multi family home? duplex? 4-plex?*

_____

_____

_____

_____

ANY ADDITIONAL INFO:

_____

_____

_____

_____

CLIENT INTAKE

Date: _____

Time frame for selling/buying/renting?

_____

☐ **Buyer**   ☐ **Seller**   ☐ **Renter**   80

First & last name: _____

Contact number: _____ Home/other: _____

Mailing address: _____

Email address: _____

Property of interest: _____ (MLS#   )

If buying, are you pre-approved? _____ If, yes, with whom? _____

Lead source:
☐ Social media   ☐ Craigslist

☐ Website   ☐ Billboard sign

☐ Newspaper/magazine AD   ☐ Real estate review book

☐ Referref by client | past client | family | friend: _____

What type of property are interested in?

☐ LAND/LOTS/ACERAGE   ☐ RESIDENTIAL   ☐ COMMERCIAL   ☐ INVESTMENT

type of land? acres? aprovements?   *sq ft # of beds/ baths acres?*   *type of building? sq ft?*   *type of property? single or multi*
water? sewer? electric?   *how many rooms? improvements?*   *family home? duplex? 4-plex?*

_____

_____

_____

_____

ANY ADDITIONAL INFO:

_____

_____

_____

_____

CLIENT INTAKE

Date: _____

Time frame for selling/buying/renting?

_____

☐ **Buyer**   ☐ **Seller**   ☐ **Renter**   81

First & last name: _____

Contact number: _____ Home/other: _____

Mailing address: _____

Email address: _____

Property of interest: _____ (MLS#   )

If buying, are you pre-approved? _____ If, yes, with whom? _____

Lead source: ☐ Social media   ☐ Craigslist

☐ Website   ☐ Billboard sign

☐ Newspaper/magazine AD   ☐ Real estate review book

☐ Referref by client | past client | family | friend: _____

What type of property are interested in?

☐ LAND/LOTS/ACERAGE   ☐ RESIDENTIAL   ☐ COMMERCIAL   ☐ INVESTMENT

type of land? acres? aprovements? water? sewer? electric? | sq ft # of beds/ baths acres? | type of building? sq ft? how many rooms? improvements? | type of property? single or multi family home? duplex? 4-plex?

_____

_____

_____

_____

ANY ADDITIONAL INFO:

_____

_____

_____

_____

CLIENT INTAKE

Date: _____

Time frame for selling/buying/renting?

_____

☐ **Buyer**   ☐ **Seller**   ☐ **Renter**   82

First & last name: _____

Contact number: _____ Home/other: _____

Mailing address: _____

Email address: _____

Property of interest: _____ (MLS# _____)

If buying, are you pre-approved? _____ If, yes, with whom? _____

Lead source: ☐ Social media   ☐ Craigslist

☐ Website   ☐ Billboard sign

☐ Newspaper/magazine AD   ☐ Real estate review book

☐ Referref by client | past client | family | friend: _____

What type of property are interested in?

☐ LAND/LOTS/ACERAGE   ☐ RESIDENTIAL   ☐ COMMERCIAL   ☐ INVESTMENT

type of land? acres? aprovements? water? sewer? electric?   sq ft # of beds/ baths acres?   type of building? sq ft? how many rooms? improvements?   type of property? single or multi family home? duplex? 4-plex?

_____

_____

_____

_____

ANY ADDITIONAL INFO:

_____

_____

_____

_____

CLIENT INTAKE

Date: _____

Time frame for selling/buying/renting?
_____

☐ **Buyer**　　　☐ **Seller**　　　☐ **Renter**　　　83

First & last name: _____

Contact number: _____ Home/other: _____

Mailing address: _____

Email address: _____

Property of interest: _____ (MLS# _____)

If buying, are you pre-approved? _____ If, yes, with whom? _____

Lead source:　　☐ Social media　　　　　☐ Craigslist

　　　　　　　　　☐ Website　　　　　　　☐ Billboard sign

　　　　　　　　　☐ Newspaper/magazine AD　☐ Real estate review book

　　　　　　　　　☐ Referref by client | past client | family | friend: _____

What type of property are interested in?

☐ LAND/LOTS/ACERAGE　　☐ RESIDENTIAL　　☐ COMMERCIAL　　☐ INVESTMENT

type of land? acres? aprovements? water? sewer? electric?　*sq ft # of beds/ baths acres?*　*type of building? sq ft? how many rooms? improvements?*　*type of property? single or multi family home? duplex? 4-plex?*

_____

_____

_____

_____

ANY ADDITIONAL INFO:

_____

_____

_____

_____

CLIENT INTAKE

Date: _____

Time frame for selling/buying/renting?

_____

☐ **Buyer**　　　☐ **Seller**　　　☐ **Renter**　　　84

First & last name: _____

Contact number: _____ Home/other: _____

Mailing address: _____

Email address: _____

Property of interest: _____ (MLS#　　　　)

If buying, are you pre-approved? _____ If, yes, with whom? _____

Lead source:　☐ Social media　　　　☐ Craigslist

　　　　　　　　☐ Website　　　　　　☐ Billboard sign

　　　　　　　　☐ Newspaper/magazine AD　☐ Real estate review book

　　　　　　　　☐ Referref by client | past client | family | friend: _____

What type of property are interested in?

☐ LAND/LOTS/ACERAGE　☐ RESIDENTIAL　☐ COMMERCIAL　☐ INVESTMENT

type of land? acres? aprovements? water? sewer? electric?　*sq ft # of beds/ baths acres?*　*type of building? sq ft? how many rooms? improvements?*　*type of property? single or multi family home? duplex? 4-plex?*

_____

_____

_____

_____

ANY ADDITIONAL INFO:

_____

_____

_____

_____

CLIENT INTAKE

Date: _____

Time frame for selling/buying/renting?

_____

☐ **Buyer**   ☐ **Seller**   ☐ **Renter**   85

First & last name: _____

Contact number: _____ Home/other: _____

Mailing address: _____

Email address: _____

Property of interest: _____ (MLS#   )

If buying, are you pre-approved? _____ If, yes, with whom? _____

Lead source:

☐ Social media   ☐ Craigslist

☐ Website   ☐ Billboard sign

☐ Newspaper/magazine AD   ☐ Real estate review book

☐ Referref by client | past client | family | friend: _____

What type of property are interested in?

☐ LAND/LOTS/ACERAGE   ☐ RESIDENTIAL   ☐ COMMERCIAL   ☐ INVESTMENT

type of land? acres? aprovements? water? sewer? electric?   *sq ft # of beds/ baths acres?*   *type of building? sq ft? how many rooms? improvements?*   *type of property? single or multi family home? duplex? 4-plex?*

_____

_____

_____

_____

ANY ADDITIONAL INFO:

_____

_____

_____

_____

CLIENT INTAKE

Date: _____

Time frame for selling/buying/renting?
_____

☐ **Buyer**   ☐ **Seller**   ☐ **Renter**   86

First & last name: _____

Contact number: _____ Home/other: _____

Mailing address: _____

Email address: _____

Property of interest: _____ (MLS# _____)

If buying, are you pre-approved? _____ If, yes, with whom? _____

Lead source: ☐ Social media   ☐ Craigslist

☐ Website   ☐ Billboard sign

☐ Newspaper/magazine AD   ☐ Real estate review book

☐ Referref by client | past client | family | friend: _____

What type of property are interested in?

☐ LAND/LOTS/ACERAGE   ☐ RESIDENTIAL   ☐ COMMERCIAL   ☐ INVESTMENT

type of land? acres? aprovements? water? sewer? electric?   sq ft # of beds/ baths acres?   type of building? sq ft? how many rooms? improvements?   type of property? single or multi family home? duplex? 4-plex?

_____

_____

_____

_____

ANY ADDITIONAL INFO:

_____

_____

_____

_____

CLIENT INTAKE

Date: _____

Time frame for selling/buying/renting?

_____

☐ **Buyer**　　　☐ **Seller**　　　☐ **Renter**　　　87

First & last name: _____

Contact number: _____ Home/other: _____

Mailing address: _____

Email address: _____

Property of interest: _____ (MLS#　　　　)

If buying, are you pre-approved? _____ If, yes, with whom? _____

Lead source:　☐ Social media　　　　　☐ Craigslist

☐ Website　　　　　　☐ Billboard sign

☐ Newspaper/magazine AD　　☐ Real estate review book

☐ Referref by client | past client | family | friend: _____

What type of property are interested in?

☐ LAND/LOTS/ACERAGE　☐ RESIDENTIAL　☐ COMMERCIAL　☐ INVESTMENT

type of land? acres? aprovements? water? sewer? electric?　*sq ft # of beds/ baths acres?*　*type of building? sq ft? how many rooms? improvements?*　*type of property? single or multi family home? duplex? 4-plex?*

_____

_____

_____

_____

ANY ADDITIONAL INFO:

_____

_____

_____

_____

CLIENT INTAKE

Date: _____

Time frame for selling/buying/renting?

_____

☐ **Buyer**   ☐ **Seller**   ☐ **Renter**   88

First & last name: _____

Contact number: _____ Home/other: _____

Mailing address: _____

Email address: _____

Property of interest: _____ (MLS# _____)

If buying, are you pre-approved? _____ If, yes, with whom? _____

Lead source:
☐ Social media   ☐ Craigslist

☐ Website   ☐ Billboard sign

☐ Newspaper/magazine AD   ☐ Real estate review book

☐ Referref by client | past client | family | friend: _____

What type of property are interested in?

☐ LAND/LOTS/ACERAGE   ☐ RESIDENTIAL   ☐ COMMERCIAL   ☐ INVESTMENT

type of land? acres? aprovements? water? sewer? electric?   *sq ft # of beds/ baths acres?*   *type of building? sq ft? how many rooms? improvements?*   *type of property? single or multi family home? duplex? 4-plex?*

_____

_____

_____

_____

ANY ADDITIONAL INFO:

_____

_____

_____

_____

CLIENT INTAKE

Date: _____

Time frame for selling/buying/renting?
_____

☐ **Buyer**   ☐ **Seller**   ☐ **Renter**   89

First & last name: _____

Contact number: _____ Home/other: _____

Mailing address: _____

Email address: _____

Property of interest: _____ (MLS#   )

If buying, are you pre-approved? _____ If, yes, with whom? _____

Lead source: ☐ Social media   ☐ Craigslist

☐ Website   ☐ Billboard sign

☐ Newspaper/magazine AD   ☐ Real estate review book

☐ Referref by client | past client | family | friend: _____

What type of property are interested in?

☐ LAND/LOTS/ACERAGE   ☐ RESIDENTIAL   ☐ COMMERCIAL   ☐ INVESTMENT

type of land? acres? aprovements? water? sewer? electric? | *sq ft # of beds/ baths acres?* | *type of building? sq ft? how many rooms? improvements?* | *type of property? single or multi family home? duplex? 4-plex?*

_____

_____

_____

_____

ANY ADDITIONAL INFO:

_____

_____

_____

_____

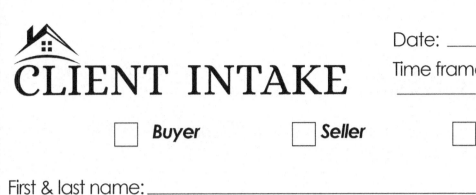

CLIENT INTAKE

Date: _____

Time frame for selling/buying/renting?

_____

☐ **Buyer**   ☐ **Seller**   ☐ **Renter**   90

First & last name: _____

Contact number: _____ Home/other: _____

Mailing address: _____

Email address: _____

Property of interest: _____ (MLS#   )

If buying, are you pre-approved? _____ If, yes, with whom? _____

Lead source: ☐ Social media   ☐ Craigslist

☐ Website   ☐ Billboard sign

☐ Newspaper/magazine AD   ☐ Real estate review book

☐ Referref by client | past client | family | friend: _____

What type of property are interested in?

☐ LAND/LOTS/ACERAGE   ☐ RESIDENTIAL   ☐ COMMERCIAL   ☐ INVESTMENT

type of land? acres? aprovements?   sq ft # of beds/ baths acres?   type of building? sq ft?   type of property? single or multi
water? sewer? electric?   how many rooms? improvements?   family home? duplex? 4-plex?

_____

_____

_____

_____

ANY ADDITIONAL INFO:

_____

_____

_____

_____

CLIENT INTAKE

Date: _____

Time frame for selling/buying/renting?

_____

☐ **Buyer**　　　　☐ **Seller**　　　　☐ **Renter**　　91

First & last name: _____

Contact number: _____ Home/other: _____

Mailing address: _____

Email address: _____

Property of interest: _____ (MLS# _____)

If buying, are you pre-approved? _____ If, yes, with whom? _____

Lead source:　☐ Social media　　　　☐ Craigslist

　　　　　　　☐ Website　　　　　　☐ Billboard sign

　　　　　　　☐ Newspaper/magazine AD　☐ Real estate review book

　　　　　　　☐ Referref by client | past client | family | friend: _____

What type of property are interested in?

☐ LAND/LOTS/ACERAGE　　☐ RESIDENTIAL　　☐ COMMERCIAL　　☐ INVESTMENT

type of land? acres? aprovements? water? sewer? electric?　*sq ft # of beds/ baths acres?*　*type of building? sq ft? how many rooms? improvements?*　*type of property? single or multi family home? duplex? 4-plex?*

_____

_____

_____

_____

ANY ADDITIONAL INFO:

_____

_____

_____

_____

CLIENT INTAKE

Date: _____

Time frame for selling/buying/renting?
_____

☐ **Buyer**　　　☐ **Seller**　　　☐ **Renter**　　　92

First & last name: _____

Contact number: _____ Home/other: _____

Mailing address: _____

Email address: _____

Property of interest: _____ (MLS# _____)

If buying, are you pre-approved? _____ If, yes, with whom? _____

Lead source:　☐ Social media　　　　☐ Craigslist

　　　　　　　　☐ Website　　　　　　☐ Billboard sign

　　　　　　　　☐ Newspaper/magazine AD　☐ Real estate review book

　　　　　　　　☐ Referref by client | past client | family | friend: _____

What type of property are interested in?

☐ LAND/LOTS/ACERAGE　☐ RESIDENTIAL　☐ COMMERCIAL　☐ INVESTMENT

type of land? acres? aprovements?　sq ft # of beds/ baths acres?　type of building? sq ft?　type of property? single or multi
water? sewer? electric?　　　　　　　　　　　　　　　　how many rooms? improvements?　family home? duplex? 4-plex?

_____

_____

_____

_____

ANY ADDITIONAL INFO:

_____

_____

_____

_____

CLIENT INTAKE

Date: _____

Time frame for selling/buying/renting?

_____

☐ **Buyer**   ☐ **Seller**   ☐ **Renter**   93

First & last name: _____

Contact number: _____ Home/other: _____

Mailing address: _____

Email address: _____

Property of interest: _____ (MLS#   )

If buying, are you pre-approved? _____ If, yes, with whom? _____

Lead source: ☐ Social media   ☐ Craigslist

                  ☐ Website   ☐ Billboard sign

                  ☐ Newspaper/magazine AD   ☐ Real estate review book

                  ☐ Referref by client | past client | family | friend: _____

What type of property are interested in?

☐ *LAND/LOTS/ACERAGE*   ☐ *RESIDENTIAL*   ☐ *COMMERCIAL*   ☐ *INVESTMENT*

type of land? acres? aprovements? water? sewer? electric?   *sq ft # of beds/ baths acres?*   *type of building? sq ft? how many rooms? improvements?*   *type of property? single or multi family home? duplex? 4-plex?*

_____

_____

_____

_____

ANY ADDITIONAL INFO:

_____

_____

_____

_____

CLIENT INTAKE

Date: _____

Time frame for selling/buying/renting?
_____

☐ **Buyer**　　　☐ **Seller**　　　☐ **Renter**　　　94

First & last name: _____

Contact number: _____ Home/other: _____

Mailing address: _____

Email address: _____

Property of interest: _____ (MLS# ____)

If buying, are you pre-approved? _____ If, yes, with whom? _____

Lead source:　☐ Social media　　　　☐ Craigslist

☐ Website　　　　☐ Billboard sign

☐ Newspaper/magazine AD　　　☐ Real estate review book

☐ Referref by client | past client | family | friend: _____

What type of property are interested in?

☐ LAND/LOTS/ACERAGE　　☐ RESIDENTIAL　　☐ COMMERCIAL　　☐ INVESTMENT

type of land? acres? aprovements? water? sewer? electric?　　sq ft # of beds/ baths acres?　　type of building? sq ft? how many rooms? improvements?　　type of property? single or multi family home? duplex? 4-plex?

_____

_____

_____

_____

ANY ADDITIONAL INFO:

_____

_____

_____

_____

CLIENT INTAKE

Date: _____

Time frame for selling/buying/renting?

_____

☐ **Buyer**   ☐ **Seller**   ☐ **Renter**   95

First & last name: _____

Contact number: _____ Home/other: _____

Mailing address: _____

Email address: _____

Property of interest: _____ (MLS# _____)

If buying, are you pre-approved? _____ If, yes, with whom? _____

Lead source: ☐ Social media   ☐ Craigslist

☐ Website   ☐ Billboard sign

☐ Newspaper/magazine AD   ☐ Real estate review book

☐ Referref by client | past client | family | friend: _____

What type of property are interested in?

☐ LAND/LOTS/ACERAGE   ☐ RESIDENTIAL   ☐ COMMERCIAL   ☐ INVESTMENT

type of land? acres? aprovements? water? sewer? electric?

sq ft # of beds/ baths acres?

type of building? sq ft? how many rooms? improvements?

type of property? single or multi family home? duplex? 4-plex?

_____

_____

_____

_____

ANY ADDITIONAL INFO:

_____

_____

_____

_____

CLIENT INTAKE

Date: _____

Time frame for selling/buying/renting?
_____

☐ **Buyer** ☐ **Seller** ☐ **Renter** 96

First & last name: _____

Contact number: _____ Home/other: _____

Mailing address: _____

Email address: _____

Property of interest: _____ (MLS#   )

If buying, are you pre-approved? _____ If, yes, with whom? _____

Lead source: ☐ Social media ☐ Craigslist

☐ Website ☐ Billboard sign

☐ Newspaper/magazine AD ☐ Real estate review book

☐ Referref by client | past client | family | friend: _____

What type of property are interested in?

☐ LAND/LOTS/ACERAGE ☐ RESIDENTIAL ☐ COMMERCIAL ☐ INVESTMENT

type of land? acres? aprovements? water? sewer? electric? | *sq ft # of beds/ baths acres?* | *type of building? sq ft? how many rooms? improvements?* | *type of property? single or multi family home? duplex? 4-plex?*

_____

_____

_____

_____

ANY ADDITIONAL INFO:

_____

_____

_____

_____

CLIENT INTAKE

Date: _____

Time frame for selling/buying/renting?
_____

☐ **Buyer**   ☐ **Seller**   ☐ **Renter**   97

First & last name: _____

Contact number: _____ Home/other: _____

Mailing address: _____

Email address: _____

Property of interest: _____ (MLS#   )

If buying, are you pre-approved? _____ If, yes, with whom? _____

Lead source: ☐ Social media   ☐ Craigslist

☐ Website   ☐ Billboard sign

☐ Newspaper/magazine AD   ☐ Real estate review book

☐ Referref by client | past client | family | friend: _____

What type of property are interested in?

☐ LAND/LOTS/ACERAGE   ☐ RESIDENTIAL   ☐ COMMERCIAL   ☐ INVESTMENT

type of land? acres? aprovements? water? sewer? electric?   *sq ft # of beds/ baths acres?*   *type of building? sq ft? how many rooms? improvements?*   *type of property? single or multi family home? duplex? 4-plex?*

_____
_____
_____
_____

ANY ADDITIONAL INFO:

_____
_____
_____
_____

CLIENT INTAKE

Date: _____

Time frame for selling/buying/renting?
_____

☐ **Buyer**　　　☐ **Seller**　　　☐ **Renter**　　　98

First & last name: _____

Contact number: _____ Home/other: _____

Mailing address: _____

Email address: _____

Property of interest: _____ (MLS#_____)

If buying, are you pre-approved? _____ If, yes, with whom? _____

Lead source:
☐ Social media　　　　　　☐ Craigslist

☐ Website　　　　　　　　☐ Billboard sign

☐ Newspaper/magazine AD　☐ Real estate review book

☐ Referref by client | past client | family | friend: _____

What type of property are interested in?

☐ LAND/LOTS/ACERAGE
type of land? acres? aprovements? water? sewer? electric?

☐ RESIDENTIAL
sq ft # of beds/ baths acres?

☐ COMMERCIAL
type of building? sq ft? how many rooms? improvements?

☐ INVESTMENT
type of property? single or multi family home? duplex? 4-plex?

_____
_____
_____
_____

ANY ADDITIONAL INFO:

_____
_____
_____
_____

CLIENT INTAKE

Date: _____

Time frame for selling/buying/renting?

_____

☐ **Buyer**   ☐ **Seller**   ☐ **Renter**   99

First & last name: _____

Contact number: _____ Home/other: _____

Mailing address: _____

Email address: _____

Property of interest: _____ (MLS#   )

If buying, are you pre-approved? _____ If, yes, with whom? _____

Lead source:
☐ Social media   ☐ Craigslist

☐ Website   ☐ Billboard sign

☐ Newspaper/magazine AD   ☐ Real estate review book

☐ Referref by client | past client | family | friend: _____

What type of property are interested in?

☐ LAND/LOTS/ACERAGE   ☐ RESIDENTIAL   ☐ COMMERCIAL   ☐ INVESTMENT

type of land? acres? aprovements?   sq ft # of beds/ baths acres?   type of building? sq ft?   type of property? single or multi
water? sewer? electric?   how many rooms? improvements?   family home? duplex? 4-plex?

_____

_____

_____

_____

ANY ADDITIONAL INFO:

_____

_____

_____

_____

CLIENT INTAKE

Date: _____

Time frame for selling/buying/renting?
_____

☐ **Buyer**   ☐ **Seller**   ☐ **Renter**   100

First & last name: _____

Contact number: _____ Home/other: _____

Mailing address: _____

Email address: _____

Property of interest: _____ (MLS#   )

If buying, are you pre-approved? _____ If, yes, with whom? _____

Lead source: ☐ Social media   ☐ Craigslist

☐ Website   ☐ Billboard sign

☐ Newspaper/magazine AD   ☐ Real estate review book

☐ Referref by client | past client | family | friend: _____

What type of property are interested in?

☐ LAND/LOTS/ACERAGE   ☐ RESIDENTIAL   ☐ COMMERCIAL   ☐ INVESTMENT

type of land? acres? aprovements? water? sewer? electric? | *sq ft # of beds/ baths acres?* | *type of building? sq ft? how many rooms? improvements?* | *type of property? single or multi family home? duplex? 4-plex?*

_____

_____

_____

_____

ANY ADDITIONAL INFO:

_____

_____

_____

_____

CLIENT INTAKE

Date: _____

Time frame for selling/buying/renting?

_____

☐ **Buyer**   ☐ **Seller**   ☐ **Renter**   101

First & last name: _____

Contact number: _____ Home/other: _____

Mailing address: _____

Email address: _____

Property of interest: _____ (MLS# ____)

If buying, are you pre-approved? _____ If, yes, with whom? _____

Lead source:
☐ Social media   ☐ Craigslist

☐ Website   ☐ Billboard sign

☐ Newspaper/magazine AD   ☐ Real estate review book

☐ Referref by client | past client | family | friend: _____

What type of property are interested in?

☐ LAND/LOTS/ACERAGE   ☐ RESIDENTIAL   ☐ COMMERCIAL   ☐ INVESTMENT

type of land? acres? aprovements?   sq ft # of beds/ baths acres?   type of building? sq ft?   type of property? single or multi
water? sewer? electric?   how many rooms? improvements?   family home? duplex? 4-plex?

_____

_____

_____

_____

ANY ADDITIONAL INFO:

_____

_____

_____

CLIENT INTAKE

Date: _____

Time frame for selling/buying/renting?
_____

☐ **Buyer**　　　☐ **Seller**　　　☐ **Renter**　　　102

First & last name: _____

Contact number: _____ Home/other: _____

Mailing address: _____

Email address: _____

Property of interest: _____ (MLS#　　　)

If buying, are you pre-approved? _____ If, yes, with whom? _____

Lead source:　☐ Social media　　　　☐ Craigslist

　　　　　　　☐ Website　　　　　　☐ Billboard sign

　　　　　　　☐ Newspaper/magazine AD　☐ Real estate review book

　　　　　　　☐ Referref by client | past client | family | friend: _____

What type of property are interested in?

☐ LAND/LOTS/ACERAGE　☐ RESIDENTIAL　☐ COMMERCIAL　☐ INVESTMENT

type of land? acres? aprovements?　sq ft # of beds/ baths acres?　type of building? sq ft?　type of property? single or multi
water? sewer? electric?　　　　　　　　　　　　how many rooms? improvements?　family home? duplex? 4-plex?

_____

_____

_____

_____

ANY ADDITIONAL INFO:

_____

_____

_____

_____

CLIENT INTAKE

Date: _____

Time frame for selling/buying/renting?

_____

☐ **Buyer**   ☐ **Seller**   ☐ **Renter**   103

First & last name: _____

Contact number: _____ Home/other: _____

Mailing address: _____

Email address: _____

Property of interest: _____ (MLS#   )

If buying, are you pre-approved? _____ If, yes, with whom? _____

Lead source: ☐ Social media   ☐ Craigslist

☐ Website   ☐ Billboard sign

☐ Newspaper/magazine AD   ☐ Real estate review book

☐ Referref by client | past client | family | friend: _____

What type of property are interested in?

☐ LAND/LOTS/ACERAGE	☐ RESIDENTIAL	☐ COMMERCIAL	☐ INVESTMENT
type of land? acres? aprovements? water? sewer? electric?	sq ft # of beds/ baths acres?	type of building? sq ft? how many rooms? improvements?	type of property? single or multi family home? duplex? 4-plex?

_____

_____

_____

_____

ANY ADDITIONAL INFO:

_____

_____

_____

_____

CLIENT INTAKE

Date: _____

Time frame for selling/buying/renting?

_____

☐ **Buyer**　　　☐ **Seller**　　　☐ **Renter**　　　104

First & last name: _____

Contact number: _____ Home/other: _____

Mailing address: _____

Email address: _____

Property of interest: _____ (MLS# _____)

If buying, are you pre-approved? _____ If, yes, with whom? _____

Lead source:　☐ Social media　　　　☐ Craigslist

　　　　　　　☐ Website　　　　　　☐ Billboard sign

　　　　　　　☐ Newspaper/magazine AD　☐ Real estate review book

　　　　　　　☐ Referref by client | past client | family | friend: _____

What type of property are interested in?

☐ LAND/LOTS/ACERAGE　　☐ RESIDENTIAL　　☐ COMMERCIAL　　☐ INVESTMENT

type of land? acres? aprovements? water? sewer? electric?　*sq ft # of beds/ baths acres?*　*type of building? sq ft? how many rooms? improvements?*　*type of property? single or multi family home? duplex? 4-plex?*

_____

_____

_____

_____

ANY ADDITIONAL INFO:

_____

_____

_____

_____

CLIENT INTAKE

Date: _____

Time frame for selling/buying/renting?

_____

☐ **Buyer**   ☐ **Seller**   ☐ **Renter**   105

First & last name: _____

Contact number: _____ Home/other: _____

Mailing address: _____

Email address: _____

Property of interest: _____ (MLS#   )

If buying, are you pre-approved? _____ If, yes, with whom? _____

Lead source:
☐ Social media   ☐ Craigslist

☐ Website   ☐ Billboard sign

☐ Newspaper/magazine AD   ☐ Real estate review book

☐ Referref by client | past client | family | friend: _____

What type of property are interested in?

☐ LAND/LOTS/ACERAGE   ☐ RESIDENTIAL   ☐ COMMERCIAL   ☐ INVESTMENT

type of land? acres? aprovements? water? sewer? electric?   *sq ft # of beds/ baths acres?*   *type of building? sq ft? how many rooms? improvements?*   *type of property? single or multi family home? duplex? 4-plex?*

_____

_____

_____

_____

ANY ADDITIONAL INFO:

_____

_____

_____

CLIENT INTAKE

Date: _____

Time frame for selling/buying/renting?
_____

☐ **Buyer**   ☐ **Seller**   ☐ **Renter**   106

First & last name: _____

Contact number: _____ Home/other: _____

Mailing address: _____

Email address: _____

Property of interest: _____ (MLS# _____)

If buying, are you pre-approved? _____ If, yes, with whom? _____

Lead source:
☐ Social media   ☐ Craigslist

☐ Website   ☐ Billboard sign

☐ Newspaper/magazine AD   ☐ Real estate review book

☐ Referref by client | past client | family | friend: _____

What type of property are interested in?

☐ LAND/LOTS/ACERAGE   ☐ RESIDENTIAL   ☐ COMMERCIAL   ☐ INVESTMENT

type of land? acres? aprovements? water? sewer? electric?

sq ft # of beds/ baths acres?

type of building? sq ft? how many rooms? improvements?

type of property? single or multi family home? duplex? 4-plex?

_____

_____

_____

_____

ANY ADDITIONAL INFO:

_____

_____

_____

_____

CLIENT INTAKE

Date: _____

Time frame for selling/buying/renting?

_____

☐ **Buyer**   ☐ **Seller**   ☐ **Renter**   107

First & last name: _____

Contact number: _____ Home/other: _____

Mailing address: _____

Email address: _____

Property of interest: _____ (MLS# ____)

If buying, are you pre-approved? _____ If, yes, with whom? _____

Lead source: ☐ Social media   ☐ Craigslist

☐ Website   ☐ Billboard sign

☐ Newspaper/magazine AD   ☐ Real estate review book

☐ Referref by client | past client | family | friend: _____

What type of property are interested in?

☐ LAND/LOTS/ACERAGE   ☐ RESIDENTIAL   ☐ COMMERCIAL   ☐ INVESTMENT

type of land? acres? aprovements?   sq ft # of beds/ baths acres?   type of building? sq ft?   type of property? single or multi
water? sewer? electric?   how many rooms? improvements?   family home? duplex? 4-plex?

_____

_____

_____

_____

ANY ADDITIONAL INFO:

_____

_____

_____

_____

CLIENT INTAKE

Date: _____

Time frame for selling/buying/renting?

_____

☐ **Buyer**   ☐ **Seller**   ☐ **Renter**   108

First & last name: _____

Contact number: _____ Home/other: _____

Mailing address: _____

Email address: _____

Property of interest: _____ (MLS# _____)

If buying, are you pre-approved? _____ If, yes, with whom? _____

Lead source: ☐ Social media   ☐ Craigslist

☐ Website   ☐ Billboard sign

☐ Newspaper/magazine AD   ☐ Real estate review book

☐ Referref by client | past client | family | friend: _____

What type of property are interested in?

☐ LAND/LOTS/ACERAGE   ☐ RESIDENTIAL   ☐ COMMERCIAL   ☐ INVESTMENT

type of land? acres? aprovements? water? sewer? electric?   sq ft # of beds/ baths acres?   type of building? sq ft? how many rooms? improvements?   type of property? single or multi family home? duplex? 4-plex?

_____

_____

_____

_____

ANY ADDITIONAL INFO:

_____

_____

_____

_____

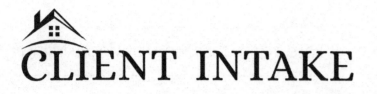

CLIENT INTAKE

Date: _____

Time frame for selling/buying/renting?
_____

☐ **Buyer**　　　☐ **Seller**　　　☐ **Renter**　　109

First & last name: _____

Contact number: _____ Home/other: _____

Mailing address: _____

Email address: _____

Property of interest: _____ (MLS# ___)

If buying, are you pre-approved? _____ If, yes, with whom? _____

Lead source:　☐ Social media　　　　☐ Craigslist

☐ Website　　　　☐ Billboard sign

☐ Newspaper/magazine AD　☐ Real estate review book

☐ Referref by client | past client | family | friend: _____

What type of property are interested in?

☐ LAND/LOTS/ACERAGE　☐ RESIDENTIAL　☐ COMMERCIAL　☐ INVESTMENT

type of land? acres? aprovements? water? sewer? electric? | sq ft # of beds/ baths acres? | type of building? sq ft? how many rooms? improvements? | type of property? single or multi family home? duplex? 4-plex?

_____

_____

_____

_____

ANY ADDITIONAL INFO:

_____

_____

_____

CLIENT INTAKE

Date: _____

Time frame for selling/buying/renting?
_____

☐ **Buyer**　　　☐ **Seller**　　　☐ **Renter**　　110

First & last name: _____

Contact number: _____ Home/other: _____

Mailing address: _____

Email address: _____

Property of interest: _____ (MLS# _____)

If buying, are you pre-approved? _____ If, yes, with whom? _____

Lead source:　☐ Social media　　　　☐ Craigslist

　　　　　　　　☐ Website　　　　　　☐ Billboard sign

　　　　　　　　☐ Newspaper/magazine AD　☐ Real estate review book

　　　　　　　　☐ Referref by client | past client | family | friend: _____

What type of property are interested in?

☐ LAND/LOTS/ACERAGE　　☐ RESIDENTIAL　　☐ COMMERCIAL　　☐ INVESTMENT

type of land? acres? aprovements?　sq ft # of beds/ baths acres?　type of building? sq ft?　type of property? single or multi
water? sewer? electric?　　　　　　　　　　　　　　how many rooms? improvements?　family home? duplex? 4-plex?

_____

_____

_____

_____

ANY ADDITIONAL INFO:

_____

_____

_____

_____

CLIENT INTAKE

Date: _____

Time frame for selling/buying/renting?
_____

☐ **Buyer**　　　☐ **Seller**　　　☐ **Renter**　　　111

First & last name: _____

Contact number: _____ Home/other: _____

Mailing address: _____

Email address: _____

Property of interest: _____ (MLS#   )

If buying, are you pre-approved? _____ If, yes, with whom? _____

Lead source:　☐ Social media　　　　　☐ Craigslist

　　　　　　　　☐ Website　　　　　　　☐ Billboard sign

　　　　　　　　☐ Newspaper/magazine AD　☐ Real estate review book

　　　　　　　　☐ Referref by client | past client | family | friend: _____

What type of property are interested in?

☐ LAND/LOTS/ACERAGE　　☐ RESIDENTIAL　　☐ COMMERCIAL　　☐ INVESTMENT

type of land? acres? aprovements?　　sq ft # of beds/ baths acres?　　type of building? sq ft?　　type of property? single or multi
water? sewer? electric?　　　　　　　　　　　　　　　　　　how many rooms? improvements?　family home? duplex? 4-plex?

_____

_____

_____

_____

ANY ADDITIONAL INFO:

_____

_____

_____

CLIENT INTAKE

Date: _____

Time frame for selling/buying/renting?

_____

☐ **Buyer**   ☐ **Seller**   ☐ **Renter**   112

First & last name: _____

Contact number: _____ Home/other: _____

Mailing address: _____

Email address: _____

Property of interest: _____ (MLS#   )

If buying, are you pre-approved? _____ If, yes, with whom? _____

Lead source:
☐ Social media   ☐ Craigslist

☐ Website   ☐ Billboard sign

☐ Newspaper/magazine AD   ☐ Real estate review book

☐ Referref by client | past client | family | friend: _____

What type of property are interested in?

☐ LAND/LOTS/ACERAGE   ☐ RESIDENTIAL   ☐ COMMERCIAL   ☐ INVESTMENT

type of land? acres? aprovements?   sq ft # of beds/ baths acres?   type of building? sq ft?   type of property? single or multi
water? sewer? electric?   how many rooms? improvements?   family home? duplex? 4-plex?

_____

_____

_____

_____

ANY ADDITIONAL INFO:

_____

_____

_____

_____

CLIENT INTAKE

Date: _____

Time frame for selling/buying/renting?
_____

☐ *Buyer*　　　☐ *Seller*　　　☐ *Renter*　　113

First & last name: _____

Contact number: _____ Home/other: _____

Mailing address: _____

Email address: _____

Property of interest: _____ (MLS#   )

If buying, are you pre-approved? _____ If, yes, with whom? _____

Lead source:　☐ Social media　　　　☐ Craigslist

　　　　　　　　☐ Website　　　　　　☐ Billboard sign

　　　　　　　　☐ Newspaper/magazine AD　☐ Real estate review book

　　　　　　　　☐ Referref by client | past client | family | friend: _____

What type of property are interested in?

☐ LAND/LOTS/ACERAGE　☐ RESIDENTIAL　☐ COMMERCIAL　☐ INVESTMENT

type of land? acres? aprovements? water? sewer? electric?　sq ft # of beds/ baths acres?　type of building? sq ft? how many rooms? improvements?　type of property? single or multi family home? duplex? 4-plex?

_____

_____

_____

_____

ANY ADDITIONAL INFO:

_____

_____

_____

_____

CLIENT INTAKE

Date: _____

Time frame for selling/buying/renting?

_____

☐ **Buyer**   ☐ **Seller**   ☐ **Renter**   114

First & last name: _____

Contact number: _____ Home/other: _____

Mailing address: _____

Email address: _____

Property of interest: _____ (MLS# _____)

If buying, are you pre-approved? _____ If, yes, with whom? _____

Lead source:
☐ Social media   ☐ Craigslist

☐ Website   ☐ Billboard sign

☐ Newspaper/magazine AD   ☐ Real estate review book

☐ Referref by client | past client | family | friend: _____

What type of property are interested in?

☐ LAND/LOTS/ACERAGE   ☐ RESIDENTIAL   ☐ COMMERCIAL   ☐ INVESTMENT

type of land? acres? aprovements?   sq ft # of beds/ baths acres?   type of building? sq ft?   type of property? single or multi
water? sewer? electric?   how many rooms? improvements?   family home? duplex? 4-plex?

_____

_____

_____

_____

ANY ADDITIONAL INFO:

_____

_____

_____

_____

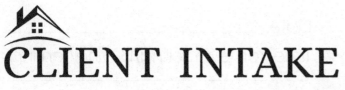

CLIENT INTAKE

Date: _____

Time frame for selling/buying/renting?
_____

☐ **Buyer**　　　☐ **Seller**　　　☐ **Renter**　　　115

First & last name: _____

Contact number: _____ Home/other: _____

Mailing address: _____

Email address: _____

Property of interest: _____ (MLS#   )

If buying, are you pre-approved? _____ If, yes, with whom? _____

Lead source:　☐ Social media　　　　☐ Craigslist

☐ Website　　　　☐ Billboard sign

☐ Newspaper/magazine AD　　☐ Real estate review book

☐ Referref by client | past client | family | friend: _____

What type of property are interested in?

☐ LAND/LOTS/ACERAGE　　☐ RESIDENTIAL　　☐ COMMERCIAL　　☐ INVESTMENT

type of land? acres? aprovements?　sq ft # of beds/ baths acres?　type of building? sq ft?　type of property? single or multi
water? sewer? electric?　　　　　　　　　　　　　how many rooms? improvements?　family home? duplex? 4-plex?

_____

_____

_____

_____

ANY ADDITIONAL INFO:

_____

_____

_____

_____

CLIENT INTAKE

Date: _____

Time frame for selling/buying/renting?
_____

☐ **Buyer**   ☐ **Seller**   ☐ **Renter**   116

First & last name: _____

Contact number: _____ Home/other: _____

Mailing address: _____

Email address: _____

Property of interest: _____ (MLS# _____)

If buying, are you pre-approved? _____ If, yes, with whom? _____

Lead source:
☐ Social media   ☐ Craigslist
☐ Website   ☐ Billboard sign
☐ Newspaper/magazine AD   ☐ Real estate review book
☐ Referref by client | past client | family | friend: _____

What type of property are interested in?

☐ LAND/LOTS/ACERAGE   ☐ RESIDENTIAL   ☐ COMMERCIAL   ☐ INVESTMENT

type of land? acres? aprovements? water? sewer? electric?   *sq ft # of beds/ baths acres?*   *type of building? sq ft? how many rooms? improvements?*   *type of property? single or multi family home? duplex? 4-plex?*

_____

_____

_____

_____

ANY ADDITIONAL INFO:

_____

_____

_____

_____

CLIENT INTAKE

Date: _____

Time frame for selling/buying/renting?
_____

☐ **Buyer**   ☐ **Seller**   ☐ **Renter**   117

First & last name: _____

Contact number: _____ Home/other: _____

Mailing address: _____

Email address: _____

Property of interest: _____ (MLS# _____)

If buying, are you pre-approved? _____ If, yes, with whom? _____

Lead source: ☐ Social media   ☐ Craigslist

☐ Website   ☐ Billboard sign

☐ Newspaper/magazine AD   ☐ Real estate review book

☐ Referref by client | past client | family | friend: _____

What type of property are interested in?

☐ LAND/LOTS/ACERAGE   ☐ RESIDENTIAL   ☐ COMMERCIAL   ☐ INVESTMENT

type of land? acres? aprovements? water? sewer? electric? | sq ft # of beds/ baths acres? | type of building? sq ft? how many rooms? improvements? | type of property? single or multi family home? duplex? 4-plex?

_____

_____

_____

_____

ANY ADDITIONAL INFO:

_____

_____

_____

_____

CLIENT INTAKE

Date: _____

Time frame for selling/buying/renting?

_____

☐ **Buyer**　　　☐ **Seller**　　　☐ **Renter**　　　118

First & last name: _____

Contact number: _____ Home/other: _____

Mailing address: _____

Email address: _____

Property of interest: _____ (MLS#　　　　)

If buying, are you pre-approved? _____ If, yes, with whom? _____

Lead source:　☐ Social media　　　　☐ Craigslist

　　　　　　　☐ Website　　　　　　☐ Billboard sign

　　　　　　　☐ Newspaper/magazine AD　☐ Real estate review book

　　　　　　　☐ Referref by client | past client | family | friend: _____

What type of property are interested in?

☐ LAND/LOTS/ACERAGE　☐ RESIDENTIAL　☐ COMMERCIAL　☐ INVESTMENT

type of land? acres? aprovements?　sq ft # of beds/ baths acres?　type of building? sq ft?　type of property? single or multi
water? sewer? electric?　　　　　　　　　　　　　　how many rooms? improvements?　family home? duplex? 4-plex?

_____

_____

_____

_____

ANY ADDITIONAL INFO:

_____

_____

_____

_____

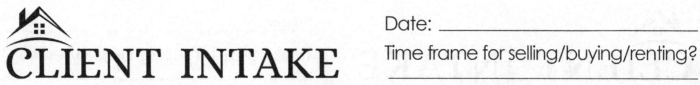

CLIENT INTAKE

Date: _____

Time frame for selling/buying/renting?
_____

☐ **Buyer**　　　☐ **Seller**　　　☐ **Renter**　　119

First & last name: _____

Contact number: _____ Home/other: _____

Mailing address: _____

Email address: _____

Property of interest: _____ (MLS# _____)

If buying, are you pre-approved? _____ If, yes, with whom? _____

Lead source:　☐ Social media　　　　☐ Craigslist

　　　　　　　☐ Website　　　　　　☐ Billboard sign

　　　　　　　☐ Newspaper/magazine AD　☐ Real estate review book

　　　　　　　☐ Referref by client | past client | family | friend: _____

What type of property are interested in?

☐ LAND/LOTS/ACERAGE　☐ RESIDENTIAL　☐ COMMERCIAL　☐ INVESTMENT

type of land? acres? aprovements? water? sewer? electric?　*sq ft # of beds/ baths acres?*　*type of building? sq ft? how many rooms? improvements?*　*type of property? single or multi family home? duplex? 4-plex?*

_____

_____

_____

_____

ANY ADDITIONAL INFO:

_____

_____

_____

_____

CLIENT INTAKE

Date: _____

Time frame for selling/buying/renting?

_____

☐ **Buyer**　　　☐ **Seller**　　　☐ **Renter**　　　120

First & last name: _____

Contact number: _____ Home/other: _____

Mailing address: _____

Email address: _____

Property of interest: _____ (MLS# _____)

If buying, are you pre-approved? _____ If, yes, with whom? _____

Lead source:　☐ Social media　　　　☐ Craigslist

☐ Website　　　　☐ Billboard sign

☐ Newspaper/magazine AD　　☐ Real estate review book

☐ Referref by client | past client | family | friend: _____

What type of property are interested in?

☐ LAND/LOTS/ACERAGE　　☐ RESIDENTIAL　　☐ COMMERCIAL　　☐ INVESTMENT

type of land? acres? aprovements? water? sewer? electric?　　sq ft # of beds/ baths acres?　　type of building? sq ft? how many rooms? improvements?　　type of property? single or multi family home? duplex? 4-plex?

_____

_____

_____

_____

ANY ADDITIONAL INFO:

_____

_____

_____

_____

Made in the USA
Las Vegas, NV
19 January 2022

41797869R00070